505 BASEBALL QUESTIONS

YOUR FRIENDS CAN'T ANSWER

JOHN KINGSTON

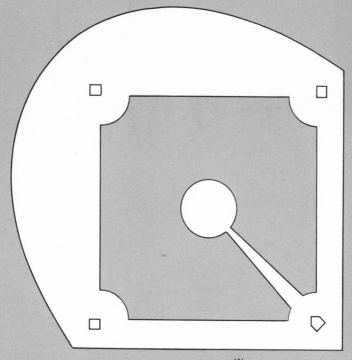

WALKER AND COMPANY NEW YORK

First published in the United States of America in 1980 by the Walker Publishing Company, Inc.

Published simultaneously in Canada by Beaverbooks, Limited, Pickering, Ontario.

Trade ISBN: 0-8027-0646-0

Paper ISBN: 0-8027-7158-0

Library of Congress Catalog Card Number: 79-56004

Printed in the United States of America

10 9 8 7 6 5 4 3 2 1

To the Original Kingston Trio:
my son, Earll John Kingston
my daughter-in-law, Maxine Hong Kingston
and my grandson, Joseph Kingston
and to my sister, Sally Baer

Contents

Pregame Warm-Up

Distances and Measurements

*Baseball Terms
and Expressions,
and Their Origins*

Distances
and Measurements

1. Fundamentally, baseballs are required for a game of baseball, so let the number one question be about a baseball. How much does a regulation baseball weigh?

2. What is the distance around a baseball (its circumference)? What is its diameter?

3. How many stitches are on a baseball?

4. What is the weight limitation of a baseball bat?

5. What is the length limitation of a baseball bat?

6. How thick can a baseball bat be?

7. The pitcher toes the rubber; what is the length and width of this white rubber?

8. What is the distance from the pitcher's mound to home plate?

9. In the previous question, I asked the distance from the pitcher's mound to home plate. How is this distance measured?

10. The distance from home to first is 90 feet and another 90 feet to second, the same to third and home—but what is the distance from third base to first base?

11. Prior to 1893, what was the distance from the pitcher's mound to home plate?

12. How wide is home plate?

13. Again, speaking of the baseball itself: How many seams are there on a baseball?

14. What is the size of a base?

15. What is the shape of the infield?

16. What is the size of the batter's box?

17. Make a guess as to the weight of the bat used by the following players:

Cobb	Williams (Ted)
Ruth	Rose
Carew	Gehrig
Bench	Aaron
DiMaggio (Joe)	Hornsby

18. As of June 1, 1958, the right and left fields of new parks and stadiums must be of certain minimum lengths. What are the minimum requirements?

19. Until 1969 the height of the pitcher's mound was 15 inches. What is it now?

20. What is the longest distance in baseball?

ANSWERS

1. *A baseball must weigh at least 5 ounces and not more than 5¼ ounces.*

2. *The circumference of a baseball is 9 inches and can be as much as 9¼ inches. Its diameter is 3 inches.*

3. *There are 216 stitches on a baseball.*

4. *There is no weight limit to a bat. Some weigh in the neighborhood of 44 ounces, others approximate 31 ounces.*

5. *A bat cannot be more than 42 inches long.*

6. *A bat cannot be more than 2-¾ inches thick.*

7. *The pitching rubber is 24 inches long and 6 inches wide.*

8. *The distance from the pitcher's mound to home plate is 60 feet, 6 inches.*

9. *The distance from the pitcher's mound to home plate begins with the front edge of the rubber and ends at the rear corner of home plate.*

10. *127 feet, 3-3/8 inches, which, of course, is also the distance from home plate to second base.*

11. *Prior to 1893, the pitcher's mound was only 50 feet from home plate.*

12. *Home plate is 17 inches wide at its greatest width.*

13. *A baseball has only one seam.*

14. *A base is 15 inches square.*

15. *The baseball infield is a square. Each side is 90 feet long. We call it a diamond. All squares are diamond shaped if you turn them, but diamond shapes are not square unless they have equal sides and 90-degree angles.*

16. *The batter's box is 6 feet by 4 feet.*

17. *Here are the bat weights of the following players.*

Ty Cobb	**38**	ounces
Babe Ruth	**44**	ounces
Rod Carew	**31**	ounces
Johnny Bench	**33**	ounces
Joe DiMaggio	**35**	ounces
Ted Williams	**32**	ounces
Pete Rose	**35**	ounces
Lou Gehrig	**34**	ounces
Hank Aaron	**33** and **34**	ounces
Rogers Hornsby	**33**	ounces

18. *All new parks and stadiums must have a minimum distance to both right and left fields of 325 feet.*

19. *The pitcher's mound has been lowered from 15 inches to 10 inches.*

20. *The longest distance in baseball (ask any pitcher) is from the pitcher's mound to the showers.*

Baseball Terms and Expressions, and Their Origins

1. You are seated at the ball park. Soon the loud speaker blares forth, "The *battery* for today's game is ..." You accept the term without giving it a thought, but why does he say *battery*? What is its origin?

2. Before the game gets underway, the pitcher warms up in the *bull pen*. Why do we say *bull* pen? Why not pig pen, cow pen, or horse pen?

3. Two games are to be played today—a *double-header*. Why do we use this expression? What is a *header* anyhow?

4. "Get your *hot dogs*!" A game wouldn't be complete without them. Why hot *dogs*?

5. We call second base the *keystone sack*. Why?

6. Did you know that the umpires didn't always use their fingers and hands in signaling balls and strikes? We take these signals for granted, but there's a definite reason why the practice started. Can you guess the origin of this custom?

7. We say *around the horn* for a double play that starts at third base. Why?

8. We stand for a *seventh inning stretch*. Wouldn't it be more logical to stand up in the fifth inning, halfway through the game? Why the seventh?

9. Why do we say *to bunt the ball*? What is the origin of the word *bunt*?

10. Lou Gehrig holds a record with twenty-three *grand slam home runs*. Where does the expression come from?

11. "The pitcher threw a *gopher ball*." Why is a home run called a *gopher ball*?

12. "Sandy Koufax pitched a *shutout*." Where did baseball pick up this expression?

13. Why do we use the term to keep *score*? Technically, a *score* is twenty ("Four score and seven years ago...").

14. A player about to bat is said to be *on deck*. Why?

15. A hit just over the head of an infielder but short of an outfielder is called a *Texas leaguer*. Why?

16. Why are some pitchers called *barbers*?

17. A player *jockeys* one on the opposing team. How did the term *jockey* get into baseball?

18. Why do we call left-handers *southpaws*?

19. All of us are baseball *fans*. Why are we called that?

20. A trio of questions for fun:

Name four musical terms found in baseball. Five?

During a baseball game, you will see two things usually found on a dining room table. If you get to the game early enough, there will be a third. What are they?

Speaking of dining, where will you find a *doughnut*?

21. Some players, most often poor hitters, bat with *a foot in the bucket*. What does this mean, and where does it come from?

22. Why are some ball players called *flakes*?

23. In every ball park you'll find a *pentagon*. Where?

24. A player makes an error by dropping the ball. We say he *muffed* it. Why?

25. A sportswriter, watching as several balls were hit sharply down the third base line, gave third base this name. What is it?

26. What is a *Baltimore chop*? How did it originate?

27. Why do we use the letter "K" to indicate a strikeout?

ANSWERS

1. *Prior to the advent of radio and television, all reports of a baseball game were sent by telegraph. The telegrapher who sent the messages and the one who received the reports were the "battery," probably because of the power that their apparatus used. In baseball the pitcher is the sender, the catcher is the receiver. In combination, they are a battery.*

2. *There are two stories as to why they say a pitcher is in the bull pen. One is that the pitcher would warm up behind a low fence, giving the impression of a bull in a pen.*

The other, to which I give more credence, is the one regarding the fence seen everywhere in rural America at that time upon which was painted a picture of a bull. This bull advertised Bull Durham tobacco for "roll-your-own" cigarettes. The pitcher warming up behind a low fence gave the appearance of being in the Bull Durham bull's pen.

3. *"There will be a double-header today." This is an old railroading expression. Sometimes it takes two locomotives at the front to pull a train. Such a two-engine train is called a "double-header." Two games of baseball, therefore, equal a double-header.*

4. *The story begins in 1900 at the Polo Grounds in New York. It was a cold April day and Harry Stevens, the head caterer, was not selling much ice cream and soda water.*

Calling his vendors, Stevens told them to go to the neighborhood markets and buy all the dachshund sausages they could find and an equal number of long rolls. (Frankfurters, which originated in Frankfurt, Germany, were called "dachshund sausages" then because of their shape.) Stevens heated the sausages and placed them in the rolls, and the vendors went through the stands shouting, "Get your red hot dachshunds!" They were an immediate success.

In the press box sat Tad Dorgan, America's number one cartoonist, searching for an idea to meet his deadline. He sketched the vendors selling red hot . . . and then stopped. *He couldn't spell "dachshunds." The next day his cartoon appeared showing the dachshund sausages in rolls, barking at one another, but for "hot dachshunds" he had substituted "hot dogs."*

Harry M. Stevens, Inc. is still feeding hundreds of thousands daily at ball parks and stadiums throughout the United States.

5. *The word "keystone" originally referred to the wedge-shaped stone at the center of an arch that held the other stones in place. Second base is the keystone sack because it is at the center of the infield.*

6. *A Player by the name of Dummy Hoy was the cause of it all. William Hoy, known as "Dummy Hoy," was deaf. He played the outfield for Washington in 1888. He could not hear the umpire's calls and asked if they would give him hand signals. They agreed and that is how it began. Dummy had a lifetime batting average of .291. He missed living to a hundred by a matter of six months.*

7. *An around-the-horn double play starts with the third baseman, goes to second base, and then to first—the long way around, so to speak. Before the Panama Canal was built, ships had to go around Cape Horn, at the southern tip of South America, to get from the east coast of the United States to the west, or vice versa.*

8. *One reason given for standing for a seventh inning stretch goes back to President Taft. He was the first president to open the season by tossing out the first ball. On this historic occasion, Taft stood up to stretch at the start of the seventh inning. Out of deference to his high office, all others followed his lead, and we have been doing it ever since.*

Another story says we stand during the seventh inning due to the luck traditionally associated with the number seven in dice.

9. *"Bunt" is another railroading term. Uncoupled freight cars are given a slight push or nudge to get them moving toward their destination. This is called "bunting." This is the same principle used in baseball; the ball is not hit but pushed or bunted.*

10. *From the game of bridge. If you take all of the tricks in bridge, you have made a grand slam. So, in baseball, if you clean the bases, you have "taken all of the runs," so to speak.*

11. *"Gopher" is a contraction of "go for." Some say it stands for "go for the fence (or the stands)," others for "go for four bases." Baseball announcers originated this use.*

12. *This expression is taken from horse racing. When a horse runs out of the money, he is "shut out." Likewise, if you come up with nothing in baseball, you have been shut out.*

13. A "score" is twenty. The shepherd taking count of his sheep would use all his fingers and toes and then make a notch, or "score," on his stick before he began over again. Thus, to count is to keep score.

14. "On deck" came from a nautically minded sportswriter.

15. A player from the Texas League, Arthur Sunday, specialized in this kind of hit to maintain a high average. (Sunday's real name was August Wacher.)

16. The term was coined by ex-Yankee pitcher Waite Hoyt. By it he meant a pitcher who talked a lot. But now it usually refers to pitchers who throw at the batter's head—close enough to shave their whiskers. Sal Maglie of the Giants and Dodgers was called "The Barber."

17. When one player taunts another, he is riding him, the way a jockey rides a horse.

18. Most baseball fields are oriented so that the pitcher throws toward the west. His left arm is, therefore, toward the south.

19. The owner of the St. Louis Browns once described an enthusiast named Charlie Haas as "the greatest of all baseball fanatics." Reporting his statement, a sportswriter shortened the word to "fan."

20. Musical terms: run, pitch, slide, and score. And then there's "base." (Ooops!)

Dining table: If you go to the ballpark early enough, you will see a pepper game. Naturally, you will find pitchers. And how about home plate?

The doughnut is a weight with a hole in the center that is slipped onto a bat to make it heavier. It is used for warm-up swings.

21. A bucket of water was always kept in the dugout or on the bench. A timid batter would place his front foot in that direction. It was said that the hitter was "putting his foot in the bucket."

Lefty Gomez, watching a rookie take batting practice and standing with his foot "in the bucket," remarked, "He bats with one foot in the [minor league] American Association." But occasionally a fine batter will adopt this stance. Al Simmons, whose lifetime average was .334, was known as "Bucketfoot Al," and both Mel Ott and Roberto Clemente stood with a foot near, if not in, the bucket.

22. Snow flakes flutter about when falling; an eccentric person is flighty. This expression originated in baseball describing a player who is uninhibited, a screwball, or who has an odd, offbeat personality.

23. *The next time you go to a ball game, have a look at the five-sided home plate.*

24. *When the game was first played, players did not use gloves. A Boston first baseman showed up with a thin protective glove one day and was ridiculed for it. His teammates said, "If you're that scared of the ball, don't play. Catch it, don't muff it." When a player fails to catch a ball, or drops it, the implication is that he is wearing a muff, which the early scoffers equated with the inventive infielder's glove.*

25. *Ren Mulford, a sportswriter, gave third base the name "hot corner" because so many hard-hit balls come that way.*

26. *The Baltimore Orioles excelled at batting a ball and making it bounce so high in the infield that the batter could reach first base before the ball could be fielded and thrown there.*

27. *Henry Chadwick devised the original scoring method for baseball in the 1850s. He used the letter "D" for a ball caught on the first bound, which was an out at that time; an "L" for a foul ball; and a "K" for a batter who struck out. Each of these is the last letter of the descriptive word: bound, foul, and struck. Only the last survives.*

The Batting Order – Plus

Babe Ruth
Mickey Mantle
Joe DiMaggio
Lou Gehrig
Hank Aaron
Ty Cobb
Willie Mays
Rogers Hornsby
Ted Williams
Stan Musial

GEORGE HERMAN "BABE" RUTH

Born: Baltimore, Maryland, February 6, 1895
• Died: August 16, 1948

1. Babe Ruth had a pet name for his big black bat. What was it?

2. His real name was George; why did we call him "Babe"?

3. Lou Gehrig's lifetime batting average was .340. Was The Babe's better or worse?

4. Early in his career, the players sawed his bats in two. What prompted them to do this?

5. The Babe had other nicknames, such as "The Sultan of Swat," "The Bambino," etc. But what was he called by his fellow players?

6. The Babe once punched an umpire in the nose. He was thrown out of the game. Within the next three hours, something happened that made the record books. What?

7. When The Babe first played for the Yankees, he replaced a player who is very well known in the sports world. His first name is also George. He was associated with the game of baseball for a very short time. Name this other George.

8. Here is an easy one. What number did Babe Ruth wear on his uniform?

9. In 1915 Babe Ruth, playing for the Red Sox, hit his first home run. That year he came within three homers of leading the league. How many did The Babe hit? Who beat him out?

10. Lou Gehrig and The Babe once encountered a young woman named Jackie Mitchell. What part did Jackie play in their lives?

11. The Babe was a practical joker. What was one thing he did to torture the rookies on his team?

12. Babe Ruth's playing was artistry personified. So, speaking of artists, just what did he have in common with two of the greatest, Michelangelo and Leonardo da Vinci?

13. In 1935 Ruth switched to the National League. On his first time at bat he faced one of baseball's immortals, Carl Hubbell. What was the result of this confrontation?

14. In 1927 The Babe hit his sixty home runs. Yankee Stadium was noted for a very short right field fence. Did Ruth take advantage of this in his record-breaking year? How many homers did he hit at home and how many on the road?

15. Hitting a home run, a triple, a double, and a single in the same game is called "hitting for the cycle." In his career, how many times did The Babe hit for the cycle?

16. Why was pitcher Hub Pruett one of Babe's greatest fans?

17. In the motion picture *Pride of the Yankees* who played the part of Babe Ruth? Who impersonated The Babe in *The Babe Ruth Story*?

18. In 1927 The Babe hit his famous sixty home runs. Who held the record that Ruth broke? What was this record, and when was it made?

19. Like Casey Stengel, The Babe had an atrocious memory for names. How did he get around this?

20. During his career, The Babe played for three teams; the Boston Red Sox, the New York Yankees, and the Boston Braves. What was the last uniform the Babe donned officially?

21. Babe's final home run during his lifetime was made off a Hall of Famer. This pitcher is as well known as The Babe himself. Name the pitcher who served up Babe's last life-time home run. (Careful!)

22. Babe led the league in hitting. He was the home run champ for many years. Strange as it may seem, he never won the Most Valuable Player Award. How come?

23. What did Babe Ruth and Hank Aaron have in common when they each hit home run number 714, aside from that fact itself?

24. As a youth at St. Mary's Industrial School, Ruth learned a trade. If he had not been a baseball player what trade could he have followed?

25. Against which team did Babe Ruth hit his first homer? Who was the pitcher? Against which team did he hit number 714? Name the pitcher.

26. Ty Cobb once had a cigarette named for him. Reggie Jackson has a candy bar. What about Babe Ruth?

27. The Babe once put on a home run hitting display before an exhibition game. Six pitchers took turns throwing balls to him. How many did he put out of the lot in an hour's time?

28. What job did Babe Ruth hold at the time of his death?

29. During World War II, Japanese soldiers paid Babe a backhanded compliment during one battle. Just how did the Japanese soldiers "honor" The Babe?

30. How many pennants had the Yankees won before Ruth joined them in 1920?

31. Babe Ruth still holds the record for having pitched the longest winning World Series game. How many innings did this game go?

32. In the Depression-haunted early thirties, Babe Ruth once demanded an $80,000 salary for the year. "Why," gasped the Yankee official, "that's more than President Hoover makes." What was The Babe's comeback?

33. Prior to 1931, a ball that hit fair and bounced into the stands was a home run. Now it's a ground rule double. In 1927, when Babe hit his sixty, how many bounced into the stands?

34. In the 1932 World Series Babe Ruth hit a home run against Charley "Cube" Root of the Cubs. It was notable for two reasons. What are they?

35. The year Babe hit sixty home runs was not his best in baseball. In what year did he hit fifty-four home runs, bat in one-hundred-thirty-seven runs, score one-hundred-thirty-seven runs, have nine triples and thirty-six doubles, and steal fourteen bases? He also batted .376 that year and had an .847 slugging average. With his .376 average he didn't lead the league; how come? Also, what did Babe slug the following year?

36. The World Series is usually played in October, yet on the 5th of September, 1918, Babe Ruth, pitching for the Red Sox, beat the Cubs in the first game of the Series, 1 to 0. How come the Series started one month early?

37. What generous act earned Babe Ruth a licking when he was only seven years old? (Hint: His friends got a licking, too, but a different kind!)

38. The pitcher who threw two home run balls to Babe Ruth in 1927 is a Hall of Famer, but you won't find him in Cooperstown. Explain; who was he?

39. One of The Babe's batted balls passed through the pitcher's legs, but it was counted as one of his sixty home runs. How come?

40. Sportswriter Fred Lieb was the first to use an expression that has been part of the Babe Ruth story for years. What is it?

41. When did Babe Ruth win the Triple Crown of batting? (Best batting average, most runs batted in, and most home runs in a single season.)

42. Ruth hit his first home run in 1915. The following year he did something that put his name in the record books. What?

43. How did The Babe have a home run taken away from him in 1918?

ANSWERS

1. *The name of Babe Ruth's bat was "Black Betsy."*

2. *It happened on his first day as a professional baseball player. Jack Dunn, manager of the Baltimore Orioles, led Ruth onto the playing field; a regular player remarked, "Here comes Jack with his newest Babe." The name stuck.*

3. *Ruth's lifetime average was .342, two points better than Gehrig's .340.*

4. *Ruth was a pitcher for the Red Sox. In those days, pitchers did not take batting practice. Defying tradition, The Babe batted with the regulars. To teach him a lesson and to show their resentment, they sawed his bats in two.*

5. *"Jidge," which was a corruption of The Babe's real first name, George.*

6. *The Babe started the game pitching for the Red Sox. He walked the first man up, Ray Morgan, on four straight balls. Babe was furious over the walk call and charged at the umpire. He cussed him out and finally punched him in the nose. Babe was tossed from the game and subsequently fined $100 and suspended for ten days. He was replaced in the game by pitcher Ernie Shore. Morgan, on first, tried to steal second and was thrown out. Ernie proceeded to dispose of the next twenty-six batters without allowing a player to reach first base. In the record book under "Perfect Games," you will find the name of Ernie Shore.*

7. *As a Yankee, Babe replaced George "Papa" Halas, owner of the Chicago Bears football team. Halas was the last right fielder for the Yankees in 1919. Incidentally, Halas hit all of .091 as a big leaguer.*

8. *Babe's number was 3. It is now retired.*

9. *In 1915 Robert (Braggo) Roth led the American League in home runs with seven. Babe Ruth had four.*

10. *The year was 1931; The Yanks were playing an exhibition game with Chattanooga. The Chattanooga pitcher was a young woman, seventeen-year-old Jackie Mitchell. She came in to pitch to The Babe, and he gallantly tipped his cap. She struck him out on five pitches. Ruth went back to the bench muttering to himself. Lou Gehrig came to the plate, took three swings at the ball, and sat down. Jackie next walked Tony Lazzeri and was taken out of the game.*

11. *The Babe made a practice of shutting rookies up in his locker.*

12. *The three of them were southpaws—left-handers.*

13. *The Babe powered one over the fence off the great Hubbell.*

14. *In 1927, the year Babe Ruth hit his sixty home runs, he hit twenty-eight at home and thirty-two on the road. The Babe wasn't too good hitting left-handed pitchers; of his sixty he hit only nineteen against the lefties.*

15. *Strange as it may seem, The Babe never hit for the cycle.*

16. *Babe Ruth was the terror of almost every pitcher he faced; but Hub Pruett of the St. Louis Browns, an otherwise undistinguished hurler, was the exception. Pruett struck Ruth out with great frequency whenever they met and once fanned him eleven times in a row.*

Pruett went on to become an obstetrician (because, he said, it was the happiest branch of medicine) and an expert performer of ragtime piano music as well as a collector of it.

17. *Babe Ruth played himself in* Pride of the Yankees, *with Gary Cooper as Lou Gehrig. William Bendix played The Babe in* The Babe Ruth Story. *As a kid, Bendix worshipped Ruth. He was a bat-boy for the Yanks and ran for hot dogs for The Babe.*

Babe Ruth wanted his movie story to be as realistic as possible, so he coached Bendix. This is the scene that took place in May, 1948, at Yankee Stadium during the filming of the picture:

The cast was to reenact Babe Ruth's sixtieth home run against Tom Zachary. Lefty Gomez, who had retired from baseball in 1944, was taking the part of Zachary. He threw to Bendix. There was a crack of the ball against the bat, and it landed over three hundred feet away, in the right field bleachers. Believe it or not, Bendix had hit a home run.

Bendix called it Babe Ruth's 715th. Lefty Gomez, shaking his head in disbelief, said he should have retired earlier.

18. *He broke his own record of fifty-nine, established in 1921.*

19. *He called every young person "Kid." The older ones were all "Doc."*

20. *The last baseball uniform worn by Babe Ruth was that of the Brooklyn Dodgers, whom he coached in 1938.*

21. *Babe's last home run was made in an exhibition game played at Yankee Stadium in 1942. The pitcher was the great Walter Johnson.*

22. *The main reason Babe never won the M.V.P. Award is that it was not given until 1931. The Babe had played seventeen years, and his best baseball was behind him. Lefty Grove with sixteen straight wins was the American League's first winner. Jimmy Foxx won it in 1932 and 1933, and Mickey Cochrane in 1934. It was Ruth's last year as a Yankee. He hit .288.*

23. *Babe hit home run number 714 as a Boston Brave, while Hank's came as an Atlanta Brave, the "grandchild" of the Boston team.*

24. *The trade Babe learned at St. Mary's Industrial School was that of tailor or shirt maker.*

25. *Babe Ruth hit his first home run against the New York Yankees. The Yankee pitcher was Jack Warhop; the year was 1915. His final home run was made on his last day in baseball and was slugged off Guy Bush pitching for the Pittsburgh Pirates at Forbes Field in Pittsburgh on May 25, 1935. He clouted homers number 712, 713, and 714 that day as he bowed out.*

26. *Babe Ruth never had a candy bar named for him. The "Baby Ruth" candy bar was named for the daughter of the President of the United States, Ruth Cleveland.*

27. *The Babe put on a slugging exhibition before a practice game at Wrigley Field, Los Angeles, 1927, the year he hit his sixty homers. He delighted the crowd by crashing 125 over the fence!*

28. *Ruth's last job was with the Ford Motor Co. He was their "Goodwill Ambassador."*

29. *During World War II, U.S. Marines, fighting in the Pacific, were startled to hear the Japanese soldiers shouting a battle cry, "To Hell with Babe Ruth!"—a left-handed tribute to The Babe.*

30. *The Yankees had never won a pennant before Babe's arrival* *in 1920. While they didn't win in his first year, they did in the next three—and many times after that, with his considerable help.*

31. *Babe is still the owner of the record for having pitched the longest winning World Series game, fourteen innings. The score was his Red Sox 2, the Dodgers, 1. The year was 1916.*

32. *"I had a better year than Hoover," he retorted.*

33. *None of Babe's sixty home runs bounced into the stands.*

34. *The homer was The Babe's famous called shot and his fifteenth and last World Series home run.*

35. *Babe's best year with the Yankees was his first, 1920. He hit for a higher average in other years but overall 1920 was his best. However, his batting average of .376 wasn't good enough to top George Sisler's .407. His slugging average tailed off to .846 in 1921, his second best year with the Yankees.*

36. *The first World War was responsible for shortening the baseball season by one month.*

37. *He stole a dollar from his father and treated his friends to ice cream cones. His reaction to the beating he got was to steal another dollar and buy his friends more cones. It didn't take long for The Babe to end up in the Industrial Home.*

38. *Ernie Nevers, Stanford's All Time All American, pitching for the St. Louis Browns, served up two round trippers to Babe during the sixty-home-run season. Ernie played pro football for the Chicago Cardinals and scored forty points in one game. He is in the National* <u>Football</u> *Hall of Fame.*

39. *Hod Lisenbee, the Washington Senators' pitcher, had a man on second and two strikes on Ruth at the plate. Tris Speaker was the Senators' center fielder. Using an old trick of his, Speaker came sneaking in trying to trap the runner off second base. He had crept to within ten feet of second base (can you imagine a center fielder doing this today?) when Lisenbee, instead of throwing to second, threw to the plate. Ruth's blow went through Lisenbee's legs. The ball nicked his pants and continued over second base. There it hit a pebble or hard spot and bounced over Speaker's head. To compound matters, the left fielder fell down. Speaker, with a pair of thirty-nine-year-old legs, went in pursuit of the ball. The Babe had no trouble circling the bases for an inside-the-park home run.*

40. *Sportswriter Fred Lieb was the first to dub Yankee Stadium, "The House That Ruth Built."*

41. *The Babe never won the Triple Crown.*

42. *In 1916, his second year in baseball, he led the American League in pitching with a 23-12 performance. This was also the year in which he won his fourteen-inning World Series game.*

43. *It happened at Fenway Park, July 8, 1918. Ruth was playing for the Boston Red Sox. Before 1920, the rule was that when the team batting last won the game in the ninth or in an extra inning, they could not win by more than one run. If a player hit a home run, which under present-day rules would have resulted in a victory by more than one run, he was given credit for a lesser hit and only the winning run counted. This happened to Ruth. He was given credit for a triple.*

MICKEY MANTLE

Born: Spavinaw, Oklahoma, October 20,1931

1. Mickey's father played amateur and semipro baseball, as did his grandfather. Mutt Mantle, as Mickey's father was known, was so determined that his son become a ball player that he named him after his own baseball hero. Who?

2. Mickey became a switch hitter at the age of ten. What prompted him to switch?

3. About how many seconds did it take Mickey to travel from home plate to first base at the height of his major league career?

4. Who was Al Benton, and what curious baseball distinction does he have?

5. How many times did Mickey win the M.V.P. Award?

6. In 1953 Mickey hit a home run at Griffith Stadium in Washington that was the longest home run ever hit. Just how far did it travel?

7. When Mickey played his first big league game for the Yankees, who were the other two outfielders?

8. We know that Mickey was the Yankee's star outfielder, but he came to the Yankees prepared to play at another position. What was it?

9. Mickey holds the World Series home run record. How many home runs did he hit in World Series competition?

10. Don Larsen's World Series perfect game against the Dodgers will be remembered forever. How did Mickey contribute to his victory?

11. The greatest one-two punch, prior to Mantle and Maris, was the combination of Ruth and Gehrig. In 1927 they produced 107 home runs between them. How many home runs did the duo of Mantle and Maris hit in 1961?

12. In 1952 Topps Bubble Gum issued a card showing the picture of Mickey Mantle. Approximately how much is this card said to be worth today?

13. Mickey jumped directly from this Class C club to the majors. Name it.

14. Mickey said this player was the best hitter he had ever seen in action. Who was he?

ANSWERS

1. *Mickey was named after the former catcher and manager Mickey Cochrane, whose real first name was Gordon. Mantle's first name is not short for Michael, but just plain Mickey.*

2. *Mickey was only ten when he became a switch hitter. His dad, a semipro right-handed pitcher, determined to make a major leaguer of his son. He began training him when Mickey was five. Mickey's grandfather was a southpaw. Mickey swung left-handed against dad and right-handed against grandpop.*

3. *Mantle was timed in 3.1 seconds going down to first. Catcher Bill Dickey, commenting on Mickey's speed, said, "You should time him going to second. Nobody who ever lived can reach second base from the plate as quickly as Mantle."*

4. *Al Benton was the only pitcher to face both Mantle and Babe Ruth in regular games. He pitched to The Babe in 1934 and to Mickey Mantle in 1952.*

5. *Mickey won the M.V.P. Award three times. Five others share this distinction: Joe DiMaggio, Jimmy Foxx, Stan Musial, Yogi Berra, and Roy Campanella.*

6. *Officially, Mickey's shot traveled 565 feet. Others have claimed longer homers, but none of them were actually measured. The ball he used is enshrined at the Baseball Hall of Fame.*

7. *Joe DiMaggio and Jackie Jensen.*

8. *Mickey was signed by the Yankees as a shortstop. He played briefly at short for the Yankees in 1953, '54, and '55.*

9. *Eighteen World Series home runs.*

10. *All Don Larsen needed in his perfect game was Mickey's home run. (Yogi Berra batted in the other run with a sacrifice.)*

11. *Between them, Maris and Mantle hit 115 home runs in 1961, the greatest one-two punch in the history of baseball.*

12. *Subject to change, Mickey's Topps Bubble Gum picture is reputed to be worth over $400.*

13. *Mickey went from the Joplin Miners to the Yankees.*

14. *Mickey thought that Ted Williams was the best hitter that he had ever seen.*

JOE DIMAGGIO

Born: Martinez, California, November 25, 1914

1. Aside from being baseball-playing brothers, the three DiMaggios have something else in common. Can you guess what it is?

2. In 1969 Joe won a poll taken by the baseball commissioner. What did he win?

3. There were nine children in the DiMaggio family. If they fielded a ball team, why would Joe naturally be the center fielder?

4. In 1949 Joe commanded a salary that was a baseball breakthrough. What was it?

5. One of DiMaggio's greatest accomplishments was hitting in fifty-six straight games. In what year did he establish this record? Whose record did he break? What was it?

6. In what year did Joe DiMaggio and Marilyn Monroe marry?

7. During DiMaggio's fifty-six-game hitting streak, how many singles did he hit? How many runs did he score? (It's easy to remember, once you know.)

8. Al Gionfriddo robbed Joe of a home run in the 1947 World Series. It was eventful to Al in another way. How?

9. Joe DiMaggio once had another stupendous hitting streak. What was it? When? Where?

10. Arch McDonald, the Yankee announcer, gave Joe his colorful nickname. What was it?

11. Brother Dom had a very respectable streak, too. What was it?

[37]

12. According to the Associated Press, seven players rated tops for baseball's first fifty years. Joe was one of the seven. Where did he stand? Who were the others?

13. What was notable about Joe's first four years in the majors?

14. In 1941, the year of his great hitting streak, DiMaggio was named the American League's Most Valuable Player. Since only one player in each league can win this award, what other great baseball feat was passed over?

ANSWERS

1. *All three have the same middle name, Paul.*

2. *Joe was named Baseball's Greatest Living Player.*

3. *He was the eighth child. (In keeping score in baseball, number eight represents the center field position.)*

4. *He was the first to receive a yearly salary of $100,000.*

5. *Joe's fifty-six-game hitting streak was made in 1941. "Wee Willie" Keeler held the old major league record of forty-four, established in 1897.*

6. *Joe DiMaggio and Marilyn Monroe were married in 1954. The marriage was dissolved in 1955.*

7. *Strange as it seems, Joe not only hit in fifty-six straight games, but he scored fifty-six runs and made fifty-six singles during the streak.*

8. *It was Al's last game in the majors. He had played four seasons.*

9. *In 1933 Joe DiMaggio hit safely in sixty-one consecutive games in the Pacific Coast League—a record for that league.*

10. *"The Yankee Clipper."*

11. *Joe's brother Dominic hit safely in thirty-four straight games. Which inspired the Boston fans to sing, to the tune of* Maryland, My Maryland, *"He's better than/His brother Joe/Dominic/DiMaggio."*

12. *Fifth. Babe Ruth was number one, Cobb number two, Gehrig number three, Walter Johnson number 4, Honus Wagner number six, and Christy Mathewson number seven.*

13. *Joe established a record by appearing on four World Series championship teams during his first four years in the majors.*

14. *Ted Williams's .406 average that year. (No one has topped Ted's .406 since then.)*

HENRY LOUIS GEHRIG

Born: New York City, June 19, 1903 • Died: June 2, 1941

1. It is June 1932. John McGraw, after managing the New York Giants for thirty years, resigns. On this same day Lou Gehrig shares the headlines with him. Why?

2. As of this writing, Gehrig still holds the record for hitting the most home runs with the bases loaded. How many grand slams did Lou hit?

3. In 1931 Lou tied Babe Ruth with forty-six home runs. Lou actually hit forty-seven, but one of them was taken away from him. What's the story behind this?

4. Gehrig holds the record for playing in the most consecutive games. What is it?

5. How did Lou's lifetime batting average compare with Ruth's?

6. Hack Wilson holds the National League record for runs batted in during a single season with 190. Lou holds the American League record. What is it?

7. Normally, a player must wait five years after retiring to become eligible for Baseball's Hall of Fame. How long after retirement was Lou elected to the Hall? Why?

8. We remember Lou for his hitting, yet in seven World Series his fielding was outstanding. Make a guess about his World Series fielding percentage.

9. One summer Lou sold insurance. Who was his first victim?

10. Babe Ruth's dramatic shot in the 1932 World Series when he pointed to the spot is remembered by all. In fact, The Babe hit two home runs in the game. What did Gehrig do in this game?

11. Lou was nicknamed "The Iron Horse" by the sports-writers, but by what name was he known to his fellow Yankees?

12. No ball player likes to make errors, but Gehrig once made a particularly embarrassing one—off the playing field. What was it?

13. After retiring from baseball, Lou held one more job before he died. What was it?

14. There was another sports champion in the Gehrig family. Who, and what sport?

15. Gehrig did not graduate from Columbia University, but he had strong connections there. What were they?

ANSWERS

1. McGraw retired from baseball on the same day Lou hit four consecutive home runs. It was the first time that a player had hit four home runs in a single game in the modern era.

2. Lou's record of twenty-three home runs with the bases loaded still stands. As of 1979, Willie McCovey was in close pursuit with eighteen.

3. It was April 26, 1931; Yankee Lyn Lary was on first when Lou hit a tremendous home run into the center-field stands. It struck a seat and bounded back onto the field. Lary thought that Rice had caught the ball and strolled toward the dugout. Gehrig crossed third after him and went on to the plate. Umpire McGowan immediately called Lou out for having passed a base runner. This made the third out. Though Lou actually hit forty-seven home runs, he had to settle for forty-six and a tie with Babe Ruth.

4. Lou played in 2,130 consecutive games from June 1, 1925 to May 2, 1939. The National League record is held by Billy Williams, 1,117 games, all played for the Chicago Cubs from 1963 to 1970.

5. The Babe's lifetime average was two points better than Lou's: .342 versus .340.

6. Lou's record of 184 runs batted in in a single season, established in 1931, is still tops in the American League. Actually it should have been two more, or 186. See question number three.

7. Lou's election to the Baseball Hall of Fame took place just a few months after his retirement from baseball, moved up because of his impending death.

8. His fielding was practically perfect in the seven World Series in which he participated. His average was .997.

9. Babe Ruth.

10. Everyone remembers Babe's dramatic gesture in the 1932 World Series and the called home run, but few remember that Gehrig also hit two home runs in the same game.

11. *"Buster."*

12. *During an appearance in a radio commercial, Lou was asked the reason for his outstanding athletic ability. "Eating Wheaties," replied Gehrig. But the cereal he was selling was Wheaties' competitor, Huskies.*

13. *He was a parole commissioner for the City of New York.*

14. *Lou's sister Adeline was a fencer and the United States foil champion from 1920 to 1923.*

15. *Lou (sometimes called Columbia Lou) waited on table, his mother cooked, and his father did maintenance work, all at Columbia University.*

"I may have been given a bad break, but I got an awful lot to live for.
"I consider myself the luckiest man on the face of the earth."

—Lou Gehrig, at a ceremony
honoring him, in Yankee Stadium
July 4, 1939

HENRY LOUIS AARON

Born: Mobile, Alabama, February 5, 1934

1. The Atlanta Braves are playing the first game of the 1974 season, at Riverfront Stadium, Cincinnati. Hank Aaron hits home run number 714, tying him with Babe Ruth. Who was the Reds' pitcher? In what inning did this occur? What was the count?

2. Willie Mays was once asked if he thought Aaron would overtake Ruth. What was Willie's reply?

3. It is 1954; Hank crashes home run number one against a Cardinal pitcher. Name the pitcher.
   But it is another pitcher who served up more gopher balls to Hank than anyone else. Who has this dubious honor?

4. There were many opinions about whether Aaron would break Babe Ruth's record. The famous Washington psychic Jeanne Dixon tried to predict the outcome. What did she say?

5. Lou Gehrig was the first to do it, then Chuck Klein, Gil Hodges, Joe Adcock, Rocky Colavito, Willie Mays, and finally Mike Schmidt. What? (Hint: Neither Aaron or Ruth ever did.)

6. When Hank came to bat in his last trip to the plate, in the final game of his career, he singled. He was replaced by a pinch runner. After the game he made a very mild protest. He had wanted to score just one more run. What was so important about this one run? (Actually, he had a legitimate beef.)

7. What was Hank's position when he first signed with the Braves?

8. Many of Hank's home runs were hit in the Atlanta stadium. Opposing pitchers dubbed the park with a not-too-complimentary nickname. Just what is this nickname?

9. Hank replaced this injured player to start his major league career. It was an exhibition game against Cincinnati. All Aaron did in this game was single, triple, and sock a home run. Whose place did he take? You know this player; he is still hated in Brooklyn and loved in New York.

10. Hank once hit a home run, but it was taken away from him. Why?

11. Babe Ruth came to bat 8,399 times during his baseball career. In this span he hit a total of 714 home runs. How many home runs did Hank Aaron hit when he had come to the plate the same number of times?

12. When Hank was in the National League, did he ever hit a home run against Cleveland in a regular season game? (Caution is advised.)

ANSWERS

1. *Jack Billingham. It was the first inning. There was no count. Aaron hit the first pitch.*

2. *Willie replied, "He's got to catch me first."*

3. *It was Vic Raschi, Cardinal pitcher, who served up the first of Hank's 755 home runs. But Don Drysdale has the doubtful distinction of having thrown more home run balls to Hank than any other pitcher. Don's contribution to Hank's record amounted to seventeen gopher balls.*

4. *She is supposed to have said, "He won't do it."*

5. *All of them hit four home runs in one game. Neither Hank nor The Babe ever did.*

6. *When Hank entered the final game of his career he was tied with Babe Ruth for career runs scored. Ty Cobb led with 2,245. Hank and Babe each had 2,174. For Hank, it would have been nice to score that final run on his last day to surpass Babe. On the other hand, he had already taken away two of the Babe's most prestigious records, most home runs and most runs batted in.*

7. *Like Mickey Mantle, Hank was signed as a shortstop.*

8. *The Atlanta stadium is called the "Launching Pad." Recently three Atlanta players hit forty or more home runs in a single season. It could be the air.*

9. *Bobby Thomson, whose home run beat the Dodgers during the 1951 National League pennant playoffs, had suffered an injury. He was replaced by the young Henry Aaron. It was the beginning of an illustrious career.*

10. *One of Hank's homers was nullified. He had stepped out of the batter's box.*

11. *Babe Ruth, 714. Aaron, 488.*

12. *His 705th home run was hit against Reggie Cleveland, St. Louis Cardinal pitcher. (Sorry!)*

TYRUS RAYMOND "TY" COBB

Born: Narrows, Banks County, Georgia, December 18, 1886
• Died: July 17, 1961

1. Ty's final year was 1928. He was forty-one. For which team did he play? At that advanced age, what was his batting average for that final year?

2. Ty's lifetime batting average is .367, the best attained by any player. The next highest average is .358. Name the player with this average.

3. Baseball's Hall of Fame opened in 1936. The first player elected was Ty, the second Babe Ruth. Who was third?

4. How does Grantland Rice figure in Cobb's life?

5. Cobb batted .420 in 1911. To what depths did Ty descend in 1912?

6. Ty was a left-handed batter. He held his right hand near the bottom of the bat. Where was his left hand when he batted?

7. The Yankees retired Babe Ruth's number. Why didn't Detroit retire Cobb's number?

8. In 1909 Cobb was the first American League player to win an outstanding award. What was it?

9. In 1961, when Cobb was dying, he checked into a hospital in Atlanta carrying a brown paper bag. What was in it?

10. Cobb once led the American League with ninety-six stolen bases. In 1950 Dominic DiMaggio led the American League in stolen bases. How many bases did Dom purloin?

11. Ty Cobb, Jackie Robinson, and Catfish Hunter all had to contend with an incurable physical disability. What is it?

12. Ty holds a record that he would have liked to forget. What is it?

13. In 1910 Cobb was given a Chalmers automobile for winning the major league batting championship. How did he enrage Mr. Chalmers?

14. Most players go through an entire season without getting five hits in a single game. Not Cobb. How many times did "the Georgia Peach" get five hits in one game in a single season?

15. Is Ty Cobb the youngest player ever to win an American League batting title?

16. How many seasons in a row did Cobb bat over .319? How does this streak fit with his overall career in the majors?

ANSWERS

1. *Ty last played for the Philadelphia Athletics. At the advanced age of forty-one, he still hit .323.*

2. *Baseball's greatest right-handed hitter, Rogers Hornsby, had a lifetime batting average of .358.*

3. *Christy Mathewson.*

4. *Grantland Rice gave Ty the nickname of "The Georgia Peach."*

5. *After hitting .420 in 1911, Cobb fell to .410 in 1912. (No major leaguer has batted .400 or over since Ted Williams's .406 in 1941.)*

6. *Ty's left hand was 4 inches above his right on the bat. He said this was the best way to hold the bat. He said it practically canceled his power, but he could do anything he wanted to with the ball. When necessary, however, Ty could really powder the ball.*
The great Honus Wagner used the same unorthodox grip.

7. *He had none. Players didn't wear numbers during Cobb's heyday. Early in the history of the game, when numbers first appeared, the fans said they made the players look like convicts, so they were removed. They reappeared in 1929; Cobb's last year was 1928.*

8. *Ty was the first American League winner of the Triple Crown. His batting average was .377. He had 115 runs batted in. He hit all of nine home runs.*

9. *One million dollars worth of negotiable securities. Cobb was a very large holder of Coca-Cola stock.*

10. *Fifteen.*

11. *All three suffered from diabetes. (Hunter, the surviving member of the trio of course still does.)*

12. *Ty Cobb made more errors than any other player in history. (After all, he had more chances than most—he played in 3,033 games.)*

13. *Cobb immediately sold his prize-winning car.*

14. *In a single season, Ty slammed out five hits in a game on five separate occasions.*

15. *If you aren't too picky, it can be argued that Al Kaline is the youngest player to win an American League batting crown. Al was born on a December 19, and Cobb on a December 18. Neither was quite twenty-one at the time. Call it a Mexican standoff.*

16. *Ty batted over .319 for twenty-three years in a row. In 1906, his first as a regular, he hit .320. He continued hitting over .319 until the end of his career in 1928, when he batted .323.*

WILLIE HOWARD MAYS

Born: Westfield, Alabama, May 6, 1931

1. Willie hit a total of 660 home runs during his fabulous career. His first was hit off a member of baseball's Hall of Fame. Name the pitcher who served up Willie's first round tripper.

2. One of baseball's latest millionaires is Cincinnati's George Foster. George hit fifty-two home runs in 1977. How does George Foster figure in Willie's record?

3. Leo Durocher was Willie's first manager. What does "The Lip" have to say about Willie?

4. In 1954 Willie made a spectacular catch in the World Series. Who hit the ball? How far did it travel?

5. Who has the higher lifetime batting average, Mays or Mickey Mantle?

6. Willie won the M.V.P. Award twice. The first time was in 1954. When did he next win this award?

7. Why was Willie known as the "Say-hey Kid?"

8. Willie holds a record for leading in one area of baseball for four consecutive years: 1956, 1957, 1958, and 1959. What did he do?

9. Willie was elected to the Baseball Hall of Fame in 1979. Surprisingly, his fans think, the vote was not unanimous. How many writers left Willie off their ballots? What percentage of ballots were cast for Mays compared to those for Ty Cobb and Babe Ruth?

10. How come Willie's cap was always falling off?

11. What was Willie's reply when asked, "Who is the best player you ever saw?" The second best, according to Mays, was who?

12. Why did the Giants have to do without Mays for part of the 1952 season and all of 1953?

13. There is one particular batting title that Willie Mays never held. Name it.

14. Joan Payson liked Willie so much that she said she would do something to keep Willie in New York. What was she willing to do?

15. How old was Willie in his first year as a Giant?

16. In the 1962 World Series' opening game, Willie scored a run off Whitey Ford that broke a streak that Whitey had established. Explain.

ANSWERS

1. *Warren Spahn of the Braves threw the ball that Willie hit for his first major league home run. The year was 1951. Willie followed that one with 659 others.*

2. *In 1969 Willie batted for Foster and clouted his 600th home run. Foster played only nine games for the Giants in 1969. He led the National League in runs batted in during 1976, 1977, and 1978.*

3. *Leo said, "For my money, he was the best."*

4. *The ball was hit by Cleveland's Vic Wertz. It traveled 460 to 475 feet.*

5. *Willie's lifetime batting average was .302. Mickey's was slightly lower at .298.*

6. *After Willie won the M.V.P. in 1954, he had an eleven-year wait before winning it again in 1965.*

7. *To quote Willie, "When I first came up to the Giants, I didn't know anybody's name. So I would holler. 'Say hey, over there!' The sportswriters picked it up."*

8. *When stolen bases are mentioned, most people think of Cobb, Brock, or Maury Wills; yet Willie led the National League in stolen bases for four consecutive years.*

9. *Twenty-three sportswriters left Willie's name off their ballots for 94.6 percent of the votes. Cobb received 98.2 percent and Ruth 95.1 percent. (How surprising that there were some writers who did not vote for these immortals, either!)*

10. *"Early in my career my cap went flying when I went to catch a ball and the fans howled. After that, I decided to play my cap loose. I guess it just became a trade mark," said Willie. Some say he always wore a cap one size smaller than his regular size.*

11. *When Willie was asked, "Who is the best player you ever saw?" he replied, "Me." (He gave second place to Pirate Roberto Clemente.)*

12. *Willie was in the service for part of 1952 and all of 1953.*

13. *Willie never led the league in runs batted in.*

14. *Joan Payson offered to buy the Giants to keep Willie in New York. The deal didn't materialize, but in 1972, after she became the owner of the New York Mets and Mays was at the end of his career, she brought Willie back to New York City.*

15. *Twenty years old.*

16. *Whitey Ford had broken Babe Ruth's World Series record of consecutive shutout innings pitched. Whitey had gone 33-⅔ innings without allowing a run. Willie broke this streak in the second inning when he crossed the plate on José Pagan's squeeze bunt.*

ROGERS HORNSBY

Born: Winters, Texas, April 27, 1896 ● Died: January 5, 1963

1. Hornsby's nickname is reminiscent of a potentate. What did they call him? Why is there an "s" after the common masculine name, Roger, in Hornsby's first name?

2. Hornsby's lifetime batting average is the second highest ever achieved. Ty Cobb's .367 leads them all. What did Rogers have?

3. The title of Hornsby's autobiography suggests constant turmoil in his baseball life. What is it?

4. Hornsby won baseball's Triple Crown in 1922 and 1925, batting over .400 each year. In 1922, in addition, he was best in another department. Name it.

5. How many times did Hornsby hit over .400 for the season?

6. Just why did Hornsby stay out of moving picture shows?

7. When you say the name "Hornsby," every fan thinks of a top hitter. Yet many considered him best in another category as well at one time. Can you guess what it was?

8. What was so unusual about Hornsby's stance at the plate?

9. How did baseball affect Hornsby's personal life?

10. One other sport seemed to take precedence even over baseball for Hornsby. What was it?

11. For the times, Hornsby made a lot of money; but he also managed to lose a lot. How?

12. When he joined the Cards in 1915, young Rogers was ignorant of baseball terminology. His manager, Miller Huggins, told him that he was going to farm him out. What did the innocent youngster do?

13. Pitchers who are being clobbered by the opposition and are about to be removed from the game sometimes try and talk the manager out of his decision. No pitcher was ever able to try this on Hornsby. Why?

14. In 1924 Hornsby set a record that could stand as long as Joe DiMaggio's fifty-six-game hitting streak. What?

15. Hank Aaron, Mickey Mantle, and Hornsby were all minor league shortstops. Rogers first came to the attention of scouts when he played short in Denison, Texas. How else did this small Texas town achieve national fame?

16. How many times in a row did Hornsby win the National League batting championship?

17. In 1933 Rogers moved over to the American League as a playing manager for the St. Louis Browns. He came to bat for the first time facing Hall of Famer Lefty Gomez of the New York Yankees. What happened?

ANSWERS

1. *"Rogers"* was transformed to *"Rajah."* Rogers was his mother's maiden name.

2. Hornsby was the greatest right-handed hitter baseball has ever known. His lifetime batting average of .358 is second to Ty Cobb's .367.

3. Appropriately, Hornsby's autobiography is titled, My War with Baseball.

4. In addition to winning the Triple Crown in 1922, he was voted the best fielding second baseman in the National League. He and Ted Williams are the only players to win the Triple Crown twice.

5. Hornsby hit over .400 three different times. In 1922 he batted .401; in 1924 it was .424, and in 1925 he hit .403.

6. A good hitter needs good eyes, and Hornsby was one of the best. He figured the movies were bad for his eyes.

7. Many will question this, but at one time he was considered to be one of the speediest runners in the National League.

8. Roger's stance at home plate was beautiful to behold. With his feet close together, he stood as far back in the right-hand corner of the box as regulations and white lines allowed.

9. Hornsby's dedication to the game was so intense that he refused to smoke, drink, or seek the companionship of women.

10. He was devoted to the Sport of Kings. He liked to play the horses. Many a time he was called on the carpet regarding his betting.

11. Not on the horses. He claimed that he broke even at the track. He took a beating playing the stock market.

12. When manager Huggins informed him that he was going to be farmed out, Hornsby obediently left for his uncle's farm.

13. *Rogers would stay in the dugout and whistle the pitcher out of the game from a distance.*

14. *Hornsby's .424 batting average in 1924 is the highest attained in modern baseball. This could remain unassailable forever. Night baseball, plus coast-to-coast travel, tend to minimize high averages.*

15. *President Dwight David Eisenhower was born in Denison, Texas, in 1890.*

16. *He won the National League batting crown six straight years, from 1920 to 1925. He also had a four-season average mark of .404.*

17. *Hornsby stepped to the plate in his first time at bat in the American League and socked Lefty Gomez's first pitch out of the lot.*

THEODORE SAMUEL WILLIAMS

Born: San Diego, California, August 30, 1918

1. How does Ted Williams's lifetime average compare with that of Joe DiMaggio, Mickey Mantle, Willie Mays, Babe Ruth, and Lou Gehrig?

2. In what decades did Ted play? For what teams?

3. Ted was called "The Splendid Splinter" by the fans. What did the ballplayers call him?

4. Ted liked a particular nickname about himself. Guess what it is.

5. One year Ted cut his own salary by $35,000. Why did he do this?

6. What gamble did Williams take on the last day of the 1941 season?

7. Carroll Hardy did something for the Red Sox that few players ever had an opportunity to do. What is it?

8. Ted had a favorite method of psyching himself up while in the batting cage. How did he do this?

9. What reason did Williams give for refusing to tip his hat to the fans after hitting a home run?

10. Ted was once fined $5,000. What was the transgression that cost Williams such a large sum?

11. Ted's mother worked for what has been called "the purest charitable organization in the world." Name it.

12. Ted's baseball career was interrupted by World War II and the Korean War. He was away for about five years. What branch of the service was he in?

13. The record for consecutive hits is twelve, held by Walt Dropo, yet Ted once reached first base more than twelve consecutive times, though not all by base hits. What was his total, and how did he attain it?

14. The date is September 28, 1960. It is the last day of Ted's memorable career. Ted comes to bat for the last time. What does he do?

15. The average person would be happy to have 20-20 vision. Ted had his vision examined by Navy doctors. What was their finding?

16. What did Ted Williams do for the Red Sox's clubhouse man, Johnny Orlando?

17. It was often said that Williams's superb eyesight, plus his natural ability, made him the superlative hitter that he was. Ted disagreed with them, saying, "You are leaving out the main reason." What had they omitted?

18. Aside from baseball, what has always been Ted's favorite pastime?

19. I have tried to steer away from statistics, but in Ted's quiz I will make an exception. What was his lifetime batting average? How many home runs did he hit? (Remember, he missed five years.) How many times did he win the batting title? In how many All-Star games did he participate? Did he ever win the M.V.P. Award?

20. What do many believe to be Ted's greatest accomplishment?

ANSWERS

1. *Ted's lifetime batting average of .344 was better than Babe's .342, Gehrig's .340, DiMaggio's .325, Mays's .302, and Mantle's .298.*

2. *Ted played in four decades. He began in 1939 and ended in 1960. His whole career was with the Boston Red Sox.*

3. *The ballplayers called Ted "The Kid."*

4. *In his autobiography Ted called himself "Teddy Ballgame."*

5. *In 1959 Ted was the highest salaried player in sports, with a yearly salary of $125,000. He suffered from a pinched nerve in his neck. It was so bad that he could hardly turn his head to look at the pitcher. For the first time in his career his batting average fell below .300. He batted only .254. He was offered the same $125,000 salary in 1960. He refused, saying that he had always been treated fairly by the Red Sox and insisted that they cut his salary the full allowable 28 percent. As a result, Ted's salary was $90,000 instead of $125,000. Incidentally, this was his last year in baseball. He hit a respectable .316. Carl Yastrzemski led the League in batting in 1968 with a .301 average.*

6. *On the last day of the season, Ted was batting .400. He could have sat out the game, protecting the .400 average. He opted to play and ended up with his .406 average.*

7. *Carroll Hardy pinch-hit for Ted in 1960. Ted had injured himself in batting practice.*

8. *Williams would get to the park early, go into the batting cage, and begin screaming at the pitcher. "I am the best ******* hitter in baseball! My name is Ted Williams! No one can get me out! I don't care who the **** you are, you can't get me out!" He would smash the ball and begin the psych job all over. It worked.*

9. *He said, "Why do they cheer me for hitting a homer and then boo me for grounding out the next time up? I'm still the same guy, ain't I?"*

10. *Ted was once fined $5,000 for spitting at the fans.*

11. *His mother was known with great affection, as "Salvation Mary." Most of her life she worked for the Salvation Army, playing the cornet in the Army's band, entertaining prisoners in the county jails. She was the champion salesperson of the Army's newspaper, War Cry.*

12. *He was a pilot for the Marine Corps.*

13. *Getting on base is what baseball is all about. Ted holds the record for having reached first safely sixteen straight times. He established this record in 1957, with six hits and ten walks.*

14. *Ted homered. It was a great climax to an illustrious career.*

15. *Navy doctors examining Ted found his vision to be 20-10, a sharpness to be found only in one person out of 100,000.*

16. *Ted gave his whole World Series check of $2,410 to the clubhouse man.*

17. *Ted said, "What they left out was that I practiced and kept on practicing."*

18. *Fishing.*

19. *Ted's lifetime batting average was .344. He hit 521 home runs. He won the batting title six times, played in eighteen All-Star games, and was voted M.V.P. twice.*

20. *Ted loved children and has donated much money and time to Boston's "Jimmy Fund." The Jimmy Fund has raised close to fourteen million dollars for research to help cancer-stricken children. In years gone by, whenever he was asked for an autograph by a prosperous-looking gentleman, Ted would ask for a check for any amount, from a dollar up, which he would immediately endorse over to the Jimmy Fund. When the check cleared, the fan had Ted's signature on the back of the check. Ted always visits these children and turns much of his television personal appearance money over to the Fund.*

STANLEY FRANK MUSIAL

Born: Donora, Pennsylvania, November 21, 1920

1. In what position did Stan begin his baseball career? What was his major league record in this position?

2. During his career, Ty Cobb got a total of 4,191 hits, which is the record. Hank Aaron, playing in both leagues, accumulated 3,771 hits. How many did Stan get, playing only in the National League?

3. Stan was discovered by Dickie Kerr, former White Sox pitcher. They became very good friends. How did Musial show his appreciation and affection for Dickie?

4. There is something very odd about the total number of hits Stan got during his career. What is it?

5. It is May 2, 1954. Stan starts hitting home runs and doesn't stop until he has established a one-day record. How many home runs did he hit in that single day?

6. Stan's first major league hit was made against a pitcher who later pitched two no-hitters in a single season. His last major league hit was against a pitcher who also pitched two no-hitters in a single season. Name the pitchers who served up Stan's first and last hits.

7. Stan always seemed to hit better against the Dodgers than any other team. The Brooklyn fans tagged him with a nickname that stayed with him throughout his career. What is this Brooklynese title?

8. Musial holds the record for extra base hits. How far behind was Babe Ruth?

ANSWERS

1. *Stan began his baseball career as a pitcher. He had pitched before coming to the majors, and his one mound appearance in the big leagues was horseplay more than anything else. His entire record consists of one pitch! (The batter was safe on an error.)*

2. *Stan accumulated 3,630 base hits.*

3. *He named his son "Richard" in honor of the great White Sox pitcher.*

4. *Of Musial's total career hits, 1,815 were made on the road and 1,815 were collected at home.*

5. *In the first game of a double-header against the Giants, Musial hit two home runs off pitcher Johnny Antonelli and one off pitcher Jim Hearn. In the second game, Stan hit two home runs off pitcher Hoyt Wilhelm. It was the first time a batter had hit five home runs in a single day.*

(At the ceremony inducting Willie Mays into the National Baseball Hall of Fame, Musial said it could have been six home runs if Mays hadn't been in the outfield for the Giants. Willie made a spectacular catch of one of Stan's long drives.)

6. *In 1941 Stan made his first major league hit against Jim Tobin. In 1944 Tobin pitched two no-hitters. One of the no-hitters was a five-inning affair; nevertheless it is in the record books.*

Jim Maloney of the Cincinnati Reds, who served up Musial's last major league hit, pitched two no-hitters in 1965.

7. *The Brooklyn fans named him "Stan the Man."*

8. *Stan holds the record for extra base hits with 1,377. Ruth's total was 1,356.*

The Game

First Inning

Second Inning

Third Inning

Fourth Inning

Fifth Inning

Sixth Inning

Top of the Seventh

Seventh Inning Stretch

Bottom of the Seventh

Eighth Inning

Ninth Inning

Extra Inning:
The Tie Breaker

First Inning

1. Willie Mays, Hank Aaron, Jackie Robinson, Roberto Clemente, and Roy Campanella are in the Black Athletes' Hall of Fame. There is one white man in the Black Athletes' Hall of Fame. Who is he, and why is he there?

2. Ask anyone to name the "Father of Baseball" and the answer will invariably be Abner Doubleday. Yet in the Greenwood Cemetery in Brooklyn, New York, you will find a tombstone on which another man's name is followed by the words "Father of Baseball." Who is that man, and why is *he* called that?

3. In the thirties a game was played that included seventeen players, both managers, and an umpire, all of whom later made the Baseball Hall of Fame. What was that game? What else was notable about it?

   The next year, another game was played in which all nine starters of one of the teams are now in the Hall of Fame. What was this game, what was the team, and who were the starters?

4. Jackie Robinson broke into the majors in 1947. What position did he play?

5. This baseball player, later a manager, started out studying dentistry but switched to baseball because he was left-handed, since only about two dentists in a hundred are left-handed. Who was this would-be dentist turned ball player turned manager?

6. Does the name Lena Blackburne mean anything to you? It should, for Lena is present at every major league game played. Who or what is Lena Blackburne?

7. What is known as the baseball players' "Bible"?

8. On a per-time-at-bat basis, Babe Ruth leads all players in the production of home runs. Who ranks second?

9. Only two major league players have played all nine positions in a regular league game. Name them.

10. Name five ways a baseball player can get on first base without hitting the ball.

11. We know Maury Wills as a base-stealer supreme, yet Maury holds an odd home run record. What did he do as a home-run hitter to get himself in the record books?

12. In 1971 a pitcher from the Phillies not only pitched a no-hitter but also hit two home runs in the same game? Who was the hurler who achieved these two nearly impossible feats in one game?

13. In his rookie year in 1911, this player hit .408. He holds the third highest lifetime batting average of .356. Only Cobb's .367 and Hornsby's .358 are higher. Yet his chances of being elected to Baseball's Hall of Fame are practically nil. Name this great but unfortunate player.

14. This catcher, making his first World Series appearance, homered his first time at bat. When he came up for the second time, he homered again. He also tied another record during the Series. Name this catcher.

15. These three brothers once played all the outfield positions for the same team in a regular major league game. Name them.

16. What player was born on a train?

17. This man hit home runs his first two times at bat in the majors. Name him.

18. Who am I? You know my name very well. As an artillery captain, I fired the first shot for the North at the beginning of the Civil War. This I did in the defense of Fort Sumter on April 12, 1861. I was a major-general and was temporarily in charge at the battle of Gettysburg. I died in 1893. My body lay in state in the City Hall in New York City and was viewed by thousands.

19. Ted Williams was our last .400 hitter. The year was 1941. Yet in 1887 eleven players hit over .400. How come?

20. Lou Gehrig holds the record for having played in 2,130 consecutive games. The National League record holder played in 1,117 games. Name him.

21. Jackie Robinson was baseball's first black player. He was a member of the Brooklyn Dodgers in the National League. Who was the first black player in the American League?

22. Lou Brock is primarily known for his outstanding speed on the bases and holds a major league base-stealing record. But in his first at-bat in the majors he didn't need speed. Why?

23. How can a team run up a total of twelve bases in a half inning and yet score no runs?

ANSWERS

1. *The white man who is in the Black Athletes' Hall of Fame is Branch Rickey. Branch made sports history in 1946 by signing Jackie Robinson. Robinson, in 1947, became the first black to play in the major leagues, opening the way for all of today's wonderful black ball players.*

2. *English-born Henry Chadwick has been called the "Father of Baseball." He wrote the first rule book in 1858. In 1869 he began publishing an annual handbook on the game that later became* Spalding's Official Baseball Guide *One of his accomplishments was developing the scoring system. He wrote for the New York* Clipper *and was the sports editor of the Brooklyn* Daily Eagle. *His signature was "Old Chalk."*

3. *The first All-Star game on July 6, 1933. Seventeen of the players are already members of the Hall of Fame, as are managers John McGraw and Connie Mack, and umpire Bill Klem.*
The next year the American League started a team of which all nine players are in the Hall of Fame: Charley Gehringer, Heinie Manush, Babe Ruth, Lou Gehrig, Jimmy Foxx, Al Simmons, Joe Cronin, Bill Dickey, and Lefty Gomez.

4. *Jackie Robinson played first base in all 151 games in his first season in the majors.*

5. *Casey Stengel gave up the idea of becoming a dentist when he learned how few left-handers there were in the profession.*

6. *The original "Lena" Blackburne was Russell Aubrey Blackburne, who was an infielder and manager in the majors from 1910 to 1929, during which he earned his misleading nickname. It probably refers to "Leapin" Lena," a popular comic strip character of the day.*
Complaints from pitchers about the difficulty of handling a slick new baseball led Blackburne to look for something to make the ball easier to grip. After several years, he discovered a distinctive mud in a body of water in Willingboro, New Jersey, and developed a

method of treating it that made it the ideal medium for his purposes. (The method is a trade secret.)

Officially named Lena Blackburne's Baseball Rubbing Mud, the product is sold in cans and still used by every professional baseball club. Before each major league game, the umpire rubs up sixty new balls with "Lena Blackburne."

Blackburne himself, while managing the Chicago White Sox in 1929, once watched with mounting exasperation as Dan Dugan, his pitcher, gave up eight straight hits to the Boston Red Sox. Blackburne finally yanked Dugan in the bottom of the eighth inning with two out. Blackburne, then forty-three and having only been an infielder during his whole playing career, proceeded to astonish the fans by taking the mound himself.

The opposing Red Sox hitter, Jack Rothrock, promptly rapped out the ninth hit but was thrown out trying to stretch, ending the inning. The White Sox lost, 17-2, and that was the end of Blackburne's pitching career. He died in 1968, but his mud goes on.

7. *The newspaper,* The Sporting News, *is the baseball players' "Bible." It is published weekly in St. Louis, Missouri, and was formerly the* St. Louis Sporting News.

8. *On a per-time-at-bat basis, Harmon Killebrew ranks second only to Babe Ruth in the matter of hitting home runs. Harmon is fifth on the all-time home run list with 573 round trippers.*

9. *The only two major leaguers who have played all nine positions in a regular league game are Campy Campaneris and Cesar Tovar. Campy did it while playing for Kansas City in 1965, Tovar with the Minnesota Twins in 1968.*

10. *The five ways a player can get on base without hitting the ball are by:*
walking
getting hit by a pitched ball
interference by the catcher
being a pinch runner
the catcher dropping the third strike.

11. *Maury Wills, in the same game, hit a home run batting left-handed and another batting right-handed.*

12. *Pitcher Rick Wise not only pitched a no-hitter against Cincinnati but in the game slugged two home runs.*

13. *Joe (Shoeless Joe) Jackson has the third highest lifetime bat-*

ting average of all ballplayers, but his involvement in the "Black Sox" scandal is enough to keep him out of the Hall of Fame even though he played a minor part in it. Some of the Chicago White Sox players had accepted money from gamblers to throw the World Series. Jackson's failure to report this was the extent of his guilt.

In his rookie year Jackson batted .408 but failed to win the batting championship because Ty Cobb hit .420.

Babe Ruth called Jackson the greatest natural hitter he ever saw and patterned his swing after him. During the tainted Series, Joe led both teams in hitting.

14. Gene Tenace, Oakland As' second-string catcher, homered his first two times up in the 1972 World Series. This had never been done before. Gene hit only .225 as a utility man during the regular season. In the Series he hit four homers, drove in nine runs, hit .348 and slugged .913. His four homers during the series was an effort that tied him with Babe Ruth. In 1977 Reggie Jackson broke the record with five home runs.

15. The San Francisco Giants were playing the Mets in New York. In the outfield for the Giants were the Alou brothers, Felipe, Matty, and Jesus. It was a regular league game in 1963.

16. Rodney Cline Carew was born October 1, 1945, on a train en route from Gatun to Colon in the Panama Canal Zone. He was named Rodney Cline for the doctor who assisted after a midwife delivered his mother on this eventful journey.

17. Bob Nieman, St. Louis Brown outfielder, hit a home run on each of his first two times at bat in the majors. Bob played for twelve years and ended up with a lifetime batting average of .295.

18. Abner Doubleday, supposed founder of the game of baseball, fired the first shot for the North at the beginning of the Civil War and was given a hero's funeral when he died.

19. The reason we had so many .400 hitters in 1887 (eleven) was that walks counted as hits.

20. Lou Gehrig played in 2,130 consecutive games. Billy Williams holds the National League record, having played in 1,117 straight games as a member of the Chicago Cubs.

21. Larry Doby was the American League's first black ball player. He came up the same year as Jackie Robinson first played in the majors. Doby played in 29 games, Jackie in 151.

22. *Lou did something on his first at-bat in the majors that can be tied but never excelled. Lou hit the first ball pitched to him for a home run. They say records are made to be broken, but not this one. He recently joined the exalted club of players who have 3,000 or more lifetime base hits.*

23. *First man up triples and is thrown out stretching it. Second man does the same. Third man triples. The fourth singles infield. The fifth singles infield. The sixth singles, but the ball hits the runner; the runner is out. A total of twelve bases, yet not a run scored.*

Second Inning

1. Name the player who hit a home run in each of eight consecutive games (Hint: He was our only left-handed catcher.)

2. In the 1956 World Series, when Don Larsen pitched his perfect game, there were three players on the Yankees who were to become major league managers. Name them.

3. Name the oldest franchise in the majors.

4. Make a guess as to how much actual playing time is consumed in a typical baseball game.

5. As of the end of 1979, which National League team has lost the most World Series?

6. This player hit safely in all seven games of the 1956 World Series and again in all seven games in 1957 and in the first three games in 1958, a total of seventeen World Series games before being stopped by Warren Spahn. Who holds this World Series record?

7. Who has received more World Series checks than anyone else?

8. Many National League players have won the Most Valuable Player Award, but only one has won it unanimously. Name him.

9. In the poem "Casey at the Bat," how many fans were present at that tragic game?

10. Ex-Dodger manager Walter Alston played for the St. Louis Cardinals in 1936. He was a first baseman. What is his lifetime batting average?

11. Gene Tenace and Babe Ruth each hit four home runs in a World Series. They share another offensive record. Guess what it is.

12. In 1975 Ted Simmons of the St. Louis Cardinals hit a home run. When he finished circling the bases, the umpire said, "It doesn't count." Simmons hadn't passed a player; he touched all of the bases. He didn't run out of the lines. He hadn't batted out of turn, nor stepped out of the batter's box. Why didn't it count?

13. Professional baseball had a beginning, but just who was the first professional baseball player? (Hint: Many of our sporting goods are made by the firm he founded.)

14. Former president Harry Truman once wanted to be a ball player, but in those days a man who wore glasses could not participate. What job did he get instead?

15. What team has been called "the greatest baseball team of all time"?

16. If an accident were to wipe out a major league team, what would happen to the league's schedule?

17. For the first time in baseball history the opening of the 1968 baseball season was postponed. What caused the postponement?

18. What is "The Murphy" to a baseball player? Hint: They would find it tough living without it.

19. We now take night games for granted, but when and where was the first night game played?

20. Name the only player removed from a World Series game. Why?

21. Have you ever wondered just how many baseballs are used by the average team in a year? Make an approximation.

22. Charles Dillon Stengel was known as "Casey," but to many he had another nickname. What was it?

23. What undefeated heavyweight champion is connected with baseball?

ANSWERS

1. *Dale Long of the Pittsburgh Pirates, in 1956. The previous record was six in six consecutive games, held by five different batters. Dale joined that select group by hitting number six off Curt Simmons.*

He had only one at bat left in the seventh game to make it seven in seven. The suspense was something awful. Dale swung twice and missed. But the next pitch was pulverized and shot out of the park. When he crossed the plate, his teammates hoisted him on their shoulders and carried him to the dugout.

In the eighth game he caught hold of Carl Erskine's curve ball and drilled it into the right field seats.

In the eight games Long batted in twenty runs and had a .536 batting average.

2. *Yogi Berra, Billy Martin, and Hank Bauer.*

3. *The oldest franchise in the majors belongs to Cincinnati.*

4. *A sportswriter, using a stopwatch, timed a game. The actual playing time was 9 minutes and 55 seconds, even though the game lasted 2½ hours. The delays came from the pitcher shuffling around the hill, pitchers being removed from the game, batters stepping in and out of the box, etc.*

5. *The Giants have lost the most World Series in the National League—nine as the New York Giants and one as the San Francisco Giants, a total of ten.*

6. *Hank Bauer. He hit safely in seventeen straight World Series games.*

7. *Frankie Crosetti has received more World Series checks than any other person. Crosetti began pulling down World Series checks in 1932. When he left as a coach in 1968, he had drawn some twenty-three checks.*

8. *The only National League player to win the Most Valuable Player Award unanimously was Orlando Cepeda of the St. Louis Cardinals in 1967.*

9. *Five thousand fans were on hand when "Mighty Casey struck out," in "Casey at the Bat." "Ten thousand eyes were upon him, 5,000 voices cheered him."*

10. *Walt Alston, ex-Dodger manager, played for the Cardinals in 1936. He was up just for a tryout and released immediately after one time at bat. His lifetime batting average was a resounding .000.*

11. *The Babe and Gene Tenace each hit four home runs in a World Series. They share a record as far as walks are concerned. In 1926, playing for the Yankees against the Cardinals, Ruth was walked eleven times. Gene drew eleven free passes in the 1973 World Series, playing for Oakland against the Mets.*

12. *The ump took a homer away from Simmons when he discovered pine tar on the bat, above the label.*

13. *The first admittedly professional baseball player was A. J. Reach, who was paid $1,000 for the 1864 season by the Philadelphia Athletics. His firm Reach & Co. is still very large in the sporting goods business. Reach was born in London, England.*

14. *They made him the umpire!*

15. *The statistics are staggering evidence that the greatest baseball team of all time was the 1927 Yankee team, which featured "Murderers' Row": Babe Ruth, who batted .356; Lou Gehrig, .373; Combs, .356; Meusel, .338; Tony Lazzeri, .309. Pitching records are equally impressive: Pennock 19-6; Hoyt, 20-7; Shocker, 18-6; and the formidable relief pitcher Wilcy Moore, 19-7. Ruth hit 60 home runs, Gehrig hit 47 and had 175 r.b.i's.*

16. *Bowie Kuhn has said, "If an accident were to wipe out a team, each remaining team in the league would make three players available to put together an instant team."*

17. *Martin Luther King's assassination on April 4, 1968, caused the postponement of baseball's opening day.*

18. *"The Murphy" is the baseball player's spring training and expense money. The name comes from Robert Murphy, a Boston attorney who gained many rights for the players in 1946.*

19. *The city in which the first night game took place was Cincinnati, in 1935. The Reds were also the first major league team to fly. The year, 1935.*

20. *Ducky Medwick is the only player ever removed from a World Series game. It happened during the 1934 World Series between the St. Louis Cards and Detroit in Detroit. It was the top of the* *sixth of the final game. The Cards were leading by a score of 7-0. Medwick came barreling into third base. He and Detroit third baseman Owen squared off. The umpires stepped in. The crowd went wild. In the bottom of the inning Medwick attempted to go to his outfield position and was greeted with apples and assorted other fruits. After going out to left field five times, Baseball Commissioner Landis called the two players, the two managers, and the chief umpire together. Court was held out on the field. Landis ordered Medwick removed for his own protection. The crowd was appeased. St. Louis won the game, 11-0, and the series.*

21. *The average team uses in the neighborhood of 10,000 baseballs a year.*

22. *Casey Stengel's mother was Irish, his father was German. Because of his German parentage he was called "Dutch."*

23. *Heavyweight champion Rocky Marciano once tried out with the Chicago Cubs as a catcher.*

Third Inning

1. The batter lines the ball over the fence; as he rounds second, he trips and sprains his ankle. What happens?

2. It is September 16, 1924. Jim Bottomley, playing for the St. Louis Cards, establishes a modern major league record for a nine-inning game. What was it, and how did he do it?

3. Joe Garagiola caught for the St. Louis Cardinals. Now there was another Garagiola who also played for the Cardinals and was related to Joe. Name this other Garagiola and the relationship to Joe.

4. This man was the Rookie of the Year. He won M.V.P. Awards in both the National and American Leagues and hit a home run for both the National League and the American League in All Star games. Name him.

5. This Hall of Famer's real name was Aloysius Szymanski. What do baseball fans know him as?

6. Only one catcher in the National League has won the M.V.P. Award three times. Name him.

7. These two catchers lived across the street from each other. One was nine months older. They were boyhood chums. One's father was a brickmaker, the other's a bricklayer. Who are they?

8. Wrestling and baseball each has had a Gorgeous George. Identify baseball's "Gorgeous George."

9. In 1968 this batter led the American League in batting with a .301 mark. It was a new low for both leagues and a far cry from Ted Williams's league-leading .406 in 1941. Name this batter.

10. What was Jackie Robinson's full name?

11. Who has been called the "Grand Old Man of Baseball"?

12. The player with the highest single season batting average in major league history was Hugh Duffy. After the season in which he hit .438, he became baseball's first famous holdout. Guess how much his raise finally amounted to.

13. How can a game be won without a winning pitcher?

14. Who won the first World Series, played in 1903?

15. Name the pitcher who lost the first World Series game ever played. His name is still widely mentioned, especially after every baseball season.

16. Most players go through an entire career without once hitting into a triple play, yet this player hit into four of them. Name him.

17. These three players entered baseball's Hall of Fame on the same day. There was a good reason for this. What was it?

18. For whom was Shea Stadium in New York named?

19. What do these Yankee numbers have in common: 3, 4, 5, 7, 8, 15, and 37?

20. Stanford University dropped their nickname, "Indians," when some of the student body protested it as a slur to native Americans. What might keep the Cleveland ball team from being asked to drop their nickname?

21. This pitcher struck out more National League batters during his career than any other. Name him.

22. At the end of 1979, Manny Mota led the National League in pinch hits with 147. Name the National League catcher whose record he broke.

23. Name the catcher who invented shin guards.

ANSWERS

1. *If a player hits a ball over the fence and trips and sprains his ankle while rounding the bases, the umpire declares the ball dead. A substitute runner may be used to complete the circuit.*

2. *He batted in twelve runs in a single game. It is still the major league record. Bottomley hit three singles, a double, and two home runs.*

3. *The other Garagiola was Joe's nice wife, who played the organ at the St. Louis Stadium.*

4. *Frank Robinson won the M.V.P. in both the American and the National Leagues. He is fourth on the all time home run list with 586 home runs.*

5. *Hall of Famer Al Simmons's real name was Aloysius Szymanski. Simmons's lifetime batting average was a hefty .334.*

6. *Roy Campanella. Campy caught for the Dodgers for ten seasons, 1948 through 1957, when he had the automobile accident that ended his career. He played in five World Series.*

7. *Yogi Berra and Joe Garagiola lived across the street from one another in St. Louis, Missouri, They were boyhood pals.*

8. *"Gorgeous George" was the nickname of George Sisler, who for most of his career played first base for the St. Louis Browns. In 1922 "Gorgeous George" batted .420, the highest mark ever in the American League, tying him with Ty Cobb's .420 established in 1911.*
Sisler holds the major league record of hits in a single season with 257. Bill Terry and Lefty O'Doul share the National League record with 254.

9. *It was Boston's Carl Yastrzemski who led the American League in batting with a .301 average.*
Carl came to the Red Sox in 1961 as a successor to Ted Williams, whose last year was 1960. He was quite shaken with the thought that he was replacing the man whom he worshipped as the greatest hitter who ever lived. Ted gave Yaz special hitting lessons, and before long Yaz came into his own.

10. *Jack Roosevelt Robinson. Jackie led the Dodgers to the pennant and was voted Rookie of the Year in 1947. In 1949 Jackie led the National League in batting, hitting .342.*

A movie was made of his life in 1950, starring Jackie himself.

Jackie led the way for blacks in major league baseball, and today 19 percent of all major leaguers are black. The National League's Most Valuable Player Award has been won by blacks over 50 percent of the time since Jackie's admittance.

11. *Branch Rickey is known as the "Grand Old Man of Baseball." He managed the St. Louis Browns and the St. Louis Cardinals and was general manager of the Brooklyn Dodgers and Pittsburgh Pirates. It was Rickey who inaugurated the farm system as a device for training and acquiring young players.*

12. *Hugh Duffy's raise amounted to $12.50 a month—$150 for the year. His .438 is the highest batting average ever recorded since the modern pitching distance was adopted.*

13. *There are no winning or losing pitchers if the game is forfeited.*

14. *The two opposing teams in the first World Series, played in 1903, were the Pittsburgh Pirates and the Boston Red Sox. The first three games were played in Boston. Boston won the Series five games to three.*

15. *The losing pitcher in the very first World Series game ever played was Boston's Cy Young. The winner was Pittsburgh's Charles Phillippe.*

16. *Brooks Robinson. In 1964 Brooks won the M.V.P. Award. He was called the "Human Vacuum Cleaner." In 1969 he was selected as the Oriole fans' all-time favorite.*

17. *The Cubs famous double-play combination, Tinker, Evers, and Chance. How could you separate Tinker-to-Evers-to-Chance in the fan's memory?*

18. *Shea Stadium was named for Bill Shea, the New York lawyer who was instrumental in returning National League baseball to New York City after the Giants and Dodgers had gone to the West Coast.*

19. *The Yankees have retired Babe Ruth's number 3, Lou Gehrig's number 4, Joe DiMaggio's number 5, Mickey Mantle's number 7, Bill Dickey's and Yogi Berra's number 8, Thurman Munson's number 15, and Casey Stengel's number 37.*

20. *In 1915 a local daily newspaper ran a contest and the name "Indians" was suggested by a fan to honor the first native American to play major league ball, Louis Francis Sockalexis. He was known as the "Chief." Sockalexis played three seasons for Cleveland. In his best year he batted .331.*

21. *Pitcher Bob Gibson holds the lifetime National League strike-out record with 3,117. Walter Johnson's American League total is 3,508.*

22. *Smoky Burgess, catcher from 1949 through 1966, held the record in the majors for pinch hits, with 144.*

23. *Shin guards are reputed to have been invented by Roger Bresnahan in 1907. At the time, most catchers would not wear them openly. They concealed them underneath their stockings.*

Fourth Inning

1. Before they were the Yankees they were the Highlanders. How did the name change?

2. Before they were the Pirates what was the name of the Pittsburgh team? And how did they get the name "Pirates"?

3. This team had two different names before their present one: the Superbas and the Bridegrooms. What do we call this team today?

4. And still on the same subject, who were the Colts?

5. What was unusual about the first baseball game ever played at the Polo Grounds in New York?

6. This man recently entered the Baseball Hall of Fame. One of his outstanding records is that of batting in 190 runs in a single season. Name him.

7. Name the two brothers who finished one and two in batting in the National League in 1966.

8. This player is not in the Hall of Fame, but his glove is. Why?

9. What was unusual about the American flag that flew over Memorial Stadium in Baltimore during the 1971 World Series?

10. Who was "Memphis Bill"?

11. My name is Earl Sheely. I broke up many games with home runs—in fact, I led the Pacific Coast League in homers. My major league lifetime batting average was an even .300. Why was I forever being kidded about my middle name?

12. Charles Dillon Stengel derived his nickname "Casey" from the fact that:
    He was born in Kansas City, Missouri.
    As a boy, he lived in Cayce, South Carolina.
    Casey's father belonged to the Knights of Columbus.
    or
    When Casey was young he used to recite the poem, "Casey at the Bat."

13. Prior to 1901 the catcher stood quite a distance behind the batter. In 1901 he was officially moved to where he is now, right behind the batter. Name the famous baseball personality who was the first to move up.

14. When Abner Doubleday founded the game, he didn't call it baseball. When did it acquire its present name?

15. In 1950, 123,707 persons crowded into Yankee Stadium What attracted this large crowd?

16. What player holds the record for having made the most hits in one game?

17. Roger Maris's sixty-first home run accomplished three things. One, you know. How about the other two.

18. This is the only player to walk up to the plate twelve times and make twelve hits. It is still the record for consecutive hits. Another player, Pinky Higgins, also made twelve hits, but his were intermingled with walks. Name this record holder.

19. This baseball great played football for Boston University. On one occasion he was sent in to punt, but instead he drop-kicked the ball 52 yards for three points. Who is he?

20. Would you believe that it is possible for a batter to hit a home run and end up catching the ball himself? It happened once. How come?

21. John McGraw, who knew a lot of ballplayers, called this man the greatest baseball player he ever saw. Many others agree.

22. Name the pitcher who allowed the most runs in a single inning (since 1900). (He later switched to the outfield and led the National League in batting twice, once hitting .398.)

23. When does a man who has quit baseball become eligible for the Hall of Fame?

ANSWERS

1. *The change came about this way: A sportswriter, not being able to fit the name "Highlanders" at the head of his column, inserted "Yankees" instead. the name stuck.*

2. *Until 1890 the Pittsburgh team was known as the Pittsburgh Alleghenies. In 1890 the Philadelphia Athletics and Pittsburgh were vying for the services of second baseman Louis Bierbauer. The Alleghenies were successful, and one of the Athletics owners, commenting on it, said vehemently, "Those Pirates!" And Pirates they've been ever since.*

3. *The Dodgers. Dodgers was originally Trolley Dodgers, which described the action of the Brooklyn players dodging the trolleys which ran on tracks directly in back of the outfield!*

4. *The Cubs were formerly called the Colts.*

5. *Both managers, John McGraw and Christy Mathewson, were arrested. The charge was violating the Blue Law that forbade Sunday baseball.*

6. *In 1930 Hack Wilson batted in 190 runs.*

7. *Matty Alou, playing for the Pirates, led the National League in 1966 in hitting with a .342 average. Right behind Matty was his brother Felipe, playing with the Atlanta Braves, who had an average of .327.*

8. *Pete Gray, whose real name was Peter Wyshner, played in the outfield for the St. Louis Browns in 1945 even though he had lost his right arm in an accident as a child. Pete played in seventy-seven games and compiled a .218 average. He had six doubles, two triples, and thirteen runs batted in.*
During World War II, so many able-bodied players were in the service that players like Pete Gray got a chance they'd never have had otherwise. But Gray was major league material by any standard. At sixteen Pete was Nanticoke, Pennsylvania's, best ball player. In 1944 he played for Memphis in the Southern Association,

where he batted .333, stole sixty-eight bases, and was named the league's most valuable player. He earned and deserved a place on a big league team.

Pete had learned to catch the ball, stick the glove under the stub of his right arm, and throw the ball in one motion. Sportswriter Joe Falls described it this way: "He'd catch the ball in that lazy easy way ball players have when they're playing catch along the sidelines."

1945 was Gray's only year in the majors—but he made it up there.

9. *The flag that flew over Memorial Stadium during the 1971 World Series was a replica of the one that flew over Fort McHenry in Baltimore during the War of 1812 when Francis Scott Key wrote "The Star Spangled Banner." It had fifteen stars and fifteen stripes.*

10. *Bill Terry's nickname was "Memphis Bill." He was the National League's last .400 hitter, batting .401 in 1930. From 1923 he was the Giant's first baseman. In 1932 Bill replaced John McGraw as manager of the Giants. He became a playing manager for the next five years, then a nonplaying manager from 1937 to 1941. Bill and Lefty O'Doul share the National League record of 254 hits in a single season. Bill's lifetime batting average of .341 rates near the top. He is in Baseball's Hall of Fame.*

11. *Home run hitter Earl Sheely's middle name was "Homer."*

12. *Charles Dillon Stengel's nickname "Casey" was derived from the initials K.C. He was born in Kansas City, Missouri.*

13. *It was Cornelius McGillicuddy, a catcher, who first moved up behind the batter. He did this before it became official in 1901. In the event you fail to recognize the name, he shortened it to Connie Mack.*

14. *Abner Doubleday founded the game in 1839 when he was twenty. At first, 4-foot-high stakes were used for what we now call bases. They were impractical, so the players switched to flat stones. One year later the stones were replaced by sacks, which were filled with sand. These became known as bases, and we had the name of the game—baseball. It was spelled "Base Ball."*

15. *Jehovah's Witnesses held their convention in Yankee Stadium for the largest crowd in its history.*

16. *The player holding the record for making the most hits in a single game is John H. Burnett. On July 10, 1932, playing for Cleveland, he made nine hits, seven of which were singles and two doubles. The only catch is that it took him eighteen innings to ac-*

complish this feat. The nine-inning record is held by Wilbert Robinson and Rennie Stennett, each of them with seven hits. Rennie's was made in 1975, "Uncle Robbie's" in 1892, playing for the Baltimore Orioles.

17. Roger Maris' s sixty-first home run gave him the home run record. It won the game for the Yankees, and it gave Maris the runs-batted-in title, beating out Jim Gentile, 142 to 141.

18. The only player to walk up to the plate twelve times and connect for twelve consecutive hits was Walt Dropo, Detroit first baseman. He did it in three games, a single game on July 14 and a double-header July 15, 1952.

19. Mickey Cochrane. Mickey's major league career spanned the years from 1925 through 1937, the last four as playing manager for Detroit. He managed Detroit in 1938 but did not play. His lifetime batting average was .320. He was selected as the catcher on the All-Time Baseball Team.

20. Dixie Walker hit a ball against the screen at Ebbets Field, Brooklyn. It stuck in the screen and was declared a home run. When Dixie went out to field his position he shook the screen, the ball came loose, and Dixie caught it—the first player to ever catch his home run ball.

21. The greatest player in baseball history, according to John McGraw, was Honus Wagner. Wagner led the National League in hitting eight times.

Honus's whole career was spent with the Pirates. In 1969 he was selected as the All-Time shortstop. His lifetime batting average was .329.

22. The pitcher who allowed the most runs in a single inning, thirteen, was Lefty O'Doul. After giving up the thirteen runs, O'Doul was sent down by the Red Sox to Salt Lake City in the Pacific Coast League, where he wisely switched to the outfield.

He earned another trial in the majors five years later and made it. He led the National League in hitting twice, once batting .398. His lifetime batting average was .349. O'Doul and Bill Terry share the National League record for the most hits in a single year, 254.

He was called "the man in the green suit" because he was a flashy dresser who favored that somewhat unconventional color. O'Doul was also known as "The Mayor of Powell Street" because of the world-famous restaurant he owned on that San Francisco thoroughfare, "Lefty O'Doul's."

23. *To be eligible for election to the Baseball Hall of Fame, a player must have been out of baseball for at least five years. There have been two players for whom that rule was waived because of special circumstances: Lou Gehrig because of his illness and impending death; Roberto Clemente after he was killed in a plane crash when still an active player—and one of the best ever.*

Fifth Inning

1. How many members of the All-Time Baseball Team selected by the Baseball Writers Association of America in 1969 can you name?

First baseman........L__ _ _____G
Second baseman.....R_____ _____Y
Shortstop ....H_____ _____R
Third baseman.......P__ _____R
Outfielder..........B____ ___H
Outfielder..........T__ ____B
Outfielder..........J__ _____O
Catcher.............M_____ _____E
Right-handed pitcher.W_____ _____N
Left-handed pitcher...L_____ _____E
Greatest player......B____ ___H
Greatest manager....J____ _____W

2. This All-Time great third baseman refused to drive an automobile. Name him.

3. How does a baseball fan learn to diaper a baby?

4. This player's failure to touch second base as the winning run scored cost the New York Giants the pennant. Name him. What nickname did this mistake earn him?

5. In a game between Detroit and Kansas City in 1972, these two brothers both worked behind the plate. How come?

6. What schools met in the first intercollegiate baseball game? What was the score?

7. Who was the youngest regular manager ever? What team did he manage? How old was he?

8. How is actor DeWolfe Hopper associated with baseball?

9. How did the San Francisco Giants (formerly the New York Giants) come by their team name?

10. In 1947 this rookie catcher hit the first pinch-hit homer in World Series history. Name him.

11. Previously, I mentioned that Henry Chadwick has been called the "Father of Baseball" and Abner Doubleday the "Founder of Baseball." Now, to confuse you a bit more, Alexander Cartwright, Jr. is called the "Father of Modern Baseball." Why?

12. Which baseball team went from last place to first place in just three weeks. When?

13. Baseball's Hall of Fame is located in Cooperstown, New York, the home of James Fenimore Cooper, author of *The Last of the Mohicans*. For whom was Cooperstown, New York, named?

14. I am reversing the normal manner of asking questions. I will give you the answer, which is "Harry Steinfeldt." Now you ask the question.

15. Most baseball followers believe that this catcher belongs in the Baseball Hall of Fame, yet the electors seem to pass him by. His nickname was "Schnozz." Who is he?

16. Name the major's first designated hitter. When did he first play this "position?"

17. Ron Hunt holds a record that really hurts. What is it?

18. Farmer Phinney printed almanacs. (His almanac became a best-seller when, because of a typographical error, snow was erroneously predicted for the Fourth of July; and strange as it seems, it actually snowed on that Independence Day.) What had Farmer Phinney to do with the game of baseball?

19. You have heard of Leo Durocher's famous remark about nice guys finishing last. In what context did he say it, and what were his exact words? *Did* they finish last?

20. Who were the opposing managers the day Bobby Thomson hit his famous home run?

21. It has been said that the baseball commissioner, Kenesaw Mountain Landis, would forgive a ball player all but one thing. What is the unforgivable action?

22. Most stadiums have artificial turf, but can you name the stadium that had it first?

ANSWERS

1. *This is the All-Time Baseball Team, selected by the Baseball Writers Association of America in 1969. It was the one hundredth anniversary of organized baseball.*

.340	*First baseman*	**Lou Gehrig**
.358	*Second baseman*	**Rogers Hornsby**
.329	*Shortstop*	**Honus (Hans) Wagner**
.320	*Third baseman*	**Pie Traynor**
.342	*Outfielder*	**Babe Ruth**
.367	*Outfielder*	**Ty Cobb**
.325	*Outfielder*	**Joe DiMaggio**
.320	*Catcher*	**Mickey Cochrane**
.414-.281	*Right-handed pitcher*	**Walter Johnson**
.300-.141	*Left-handed pitcher*	**Lefty Grove**
	Greatest player	**Babe Ruth**
	Greatest manager	**John McGraw**

2. *Baseball's All-Time third baseman, Pie Traynor, refused to drive an automobile.*

3. *First, place the diaper in the position of a baseball diamond.*
Next, fold second base over home plate.
Place the baby on the pitcher's mound.
Then pin first base and third base to home plate.
Try to keep the game from being called on account of rain.

4. *Fred Merkle's failure to touch second as the winning run scored cost the New York Giants the pennant in 1908. The game was called a tie. In the play-off for the pennant the Cubs beat the Giants. The term "Bonehead Merkle" was invented by the fans.*

5. *Tom Haller was catching for Detroit and his brother, Bill Haller, was umpiring. Gotcha that time!*

6. *The score of the first intercollegiate baseball game ever played was Amherst, 73, Williams, 32.*

7. *The youngest regular manager was Lou Boudreau, who managed the Cleveland Indians at the age of twenty-four. The year was 1942.*

Roger Peckinpaugh, age twenty-three, was a temporary manager of the Yankees in 1914.

8. *DeWolfe Hopper recited Ernest L. Thayer's poem, "Casey at the Bat," with such drama that audiences demanded it every time he appeared. Thayer wrote this minor classic in 1888.*

9. *After a victory, manager Jim Mutrie exultantly cried out, "My big fellows, my giants!" Mutrie was nicknamed "Truthful Jim"—he was never known to lie or exaggerate.*

10. *The first pinch-hit home run in a World Series game was made by Yogi Berra in 1947. It was his rookie year with the Yanks.*

11. *On his plaque in the Baseball Hall of Fame are these words: "Alexander Joy Cartwright, Jr. 'Father of Modern Baseball' set bases 90 feet apart, established 9 innings as a game and 9 players to a team. He also formed baseball's first team, the 'Knicker-bockers,' Sept. 23, 1845."*

12. *The 1973 Mets were last on August 30 and first on September 21.*

13. *Cooperstown, New York, the home of Baseball's Hall of Fame, was named for William Cooper, the father of the author, James Fenimore Cooper.*

14. *The question you should ask is: All of us have heard of the famous double-play combination, Tinker to Evers to Chance. Who was the third baseman?*

15. *Ernesto Natalie (Ernie) Lombardi was known to his team-mates as "Schnozz." Fans wonder why he was never elected to the Hall of Fame. Ernie's career spanned the years from 1931 through 1947.*

16. *Ron Blomberg of the Yankees became the first official desig-nated hitter in major league history when he walked on five pitches with the bases loaded in the first inning against the Red Sox on opening day, April 6, 1973, at Boston's Fenway Park.*

17. *Hunt led the National League in getting hit by a pitched ball for a record seven consecutive years.*

18. *When Abner Doubleday was twenty years old, he laid out baseball's first diamond on Farmer Phinney's lot in Cooperstown, New York. The first game of baseball was played there. An annual commemorative game is still played on Farmer Phinney's lot.*

19. *Leo was referring to the New York Giants with Mel Ott as manager. Leo said, "Take a look at them; all nice guys. They'll finish last. Nice guys. Finish last."*

In midseason, Leo himself took over the managership of the Giants from Ott. They finished fifth, in an eight-team league.

20. *I can't answer that question without reliving the whole exciting story of "The Miracle of Coogan's Bluff."*

In August, 1951, Leo Durocher's Giants trailed the first-place Brooklyn Dodgers by thirteen-and-a-half games; but by season's end both teams were tied for the pennant, necessitating a three-game play-off. The Giants captured the first game, 3 to 1, but were trounced, 10 to 0, in the second. The third and final game was played at the Polo Grounds (on Coogan's Bluff) on October 3, 1951.

The Dodgers are leading, 4 to 1, as we start the ninth inning; they seem to have the pennant all wrapped up. Don Newcombe is pitching for the Dodgers and has been mowing the Giants down all afternoon. Alvin Dark steps to the plate. He beats out an infield hit. The Dodger fans still have nothing to worry about.

They fidget a bit when Mueller singles, putting runners on first and third; but Monte Irvin pops out. Whitey Lockman then smacks a double, driving in Dark; and the score is now 4 to 2.

On that play Mueller has sprained his ankle sliding into third, and pitcher Clint Hartung goes in to run in his place. Dodger manager Chuck Dressen calls in Ralph Branca from the bull pen.

Bobby Thomson, the "Flying Scot," stands at the plate. Branca zooms a strike past him; but on the next pitch Bobby slams the ball into the left field stands for a home run.

Pandemonium breaks loose. The Giants win the game, 5 to 4, and with it the National League Pennant.

Anticlimax: The Giants lost the Series to the Yankees, four games to two. But their drive to first place, and the dramatic third play-off game, certainly deserves the title "The Miracle of Coogan's Bluff."

21. *Judge Landis was made Commissioner of Baseball after the "Black Sox" scandal of 1919. In later years, Landis was to say he would forgive a player practically anything but gambling.*

22. *The first stadium to have artificial turf was, logically enough, the Astrodome in Houston.*

Sixth Inning

1. Hack Wilson's real name was Lewis Robert Wilson. How did he acquire the nickname "Hack"?

2. Dizzy Dean was christened Jay Hanna, yet later in life called himself, Jerome Herman. Why?

3. Who was the captain of the St. Louis "Gas House Gang"?

4. What was unusual about the 1928 Philadelphia Athletics?

5. These children could say, "Both of our grandfathers are in Baseballs' Hall of Fame." Whose children are these?

6. When a delegation called on him to inform him of his nomination to the presidency, he was playing baseball and kept the callers waiting until he had another chance to hit. Who was this man who loved the people and the game of the people?

7. Who was catching for the Dodgers when they signed Roy Campanella?

8. Tinkers to Evers to Chance: One of the three was originally signed by the Cubs as a catcher. Which?

9. Two of the oldest parks in baseball opened on the same day, April 20, 1912. Name them.

10. Jimmy Foxx, one of baseballs' all-time greats, played first and caught for most of his career. In 1939 and again in 1945 he did something else on the baseball diamond. What did Jimmy do?

11. "Say it isn't so, Joe" is a well-known saying, but just what is its origin?

12. Name the team in the American League that has lost the most World Series.

13. This sounds like a trick question, but it isn't. How was it possible for a batter to come to the plate only once during an inning, get on with only a single, steal three bases, and not advance farther than second? This actually happened.

14. In 1970 Bobby Bonds of the San Francisco Giants established the major league record for number of strikeouts at bat for one season with 189. Whose record did Bobby better (or make worse)?

15. Junction City, a Class D team in the Central Kansas League, once had a player calling himself "Wilson." He was a good hitter, batting .355. After playing fourteen games he quit baseball for good and later went on to great fame under his true name. Name this man who assumed the name of a former president.

16. The 1908 Chicago White Sox, as someone said, "excelled in ineptitude." Make a guess as to how many home runs the club hit during the season.

17. Bucky Dent said, "Three wonderful things happened to me in 1978." Name them.

18. What connection did California Governor Reagan have with organized baseball?

19. Name the slugger who led the American League in strikeouts at bat for four consecutive years with 171, 142, 135, and 161.

20. What do Steve Garvey and Walter Johnson have in common?

21. About what perennial cellar dwellers is there a clever parody on a phrase that once honored a great American? What is it?

22. On the night of May 24, 1935, the Reds defeated the Phillies in Cincinnati. The score was 2 to 1. What was significant about this game?

23. How did the first ball players dress? The early umpires?

ANSWERS

1. *Hack Wilson's nickname was derived from the fact that in build he resembled the great Russian wrestler, George Hackenschmidt.*

2. *People might have laughed at Diz for his eccentricities, but he was quite a human being. A neighbor's friend had lost a son and was inconsolable in his grief. To comfort him, Jay changed his name, Jay Hanna, to Jerome Herman, that of the dead boy.*

3. *Leo Durocher.*

4. *The 1928 Philadelphia Athletics had the greatest collection of future "Hall of Famers" ever assembled, not counting All-Star Games. Some of the players on this team were: Ty Cobb, Eddie Collins, Tris Speaker, Mickey Cochrane, Lefty Grove, Jimmie Foxx, and Al Simmons, plus Manager Connie Mack. (But they finished second, behind the Yankees.)*

5. *Herb Pennock's daughter, Jane, married Eddie Collins, Jr. Both Herb and Eddie, Sr. are in the Hall of Fame. Herb won five World Series games without a loss. The only pitcher with a better World Series record is Lefty Gomez, with six wins and no losses.*

6. *At least temporarily, the game of the people ranked ahead of the presidency, for Abraham Lincoln let the good news wait.*

The game of baseball at the time was twenty-one years old. Many of today's rules were in force by 1860—for example, the fielder had to catch the ball on the fly for a putout; prior to 1858 he had to catch it on the first bounce.

The first organized game was played that year in San Francisco, and the first intercollegiate game (between Williams and Amherst) had been played the year before.

7. *Gilbert Raymond Hodges was the Dodgers catcher when they signed Roy Campanella. Most of Gil's career was spent playing first base for the Brooklyn team.*

8. *Frank Chance was originally signed as a catcher. He played that position for the University of California.*

9. *Tiger Stadium in Detroit and Fenway Park in Boston opened on the same day, April 20, 1912.*

10. *Jimmy Foxx pitched in 1939 and 1945. His lifetime pitching record reads, won 1, lost 0.*

11. *Joe Jackson, with the third highest batting average of all time (.356), was involved in the Black Sox Scandal. After the trial, his newsboy approached his hero and said, "Say it isn't so, Joe!"*

12. *While the Yankees have won the most World Series, they also lead the American League in the number of World Series lost, with ten. They have won twenty-two World Series.*

13. *Herman "Germany" Schaefer singled, stole second, and then turned right around and stole first base, then re-stole second. Asked why he did it, he replied, "Just to confuse the pitcher." There was nothing in the rule book forbidding it. There is now.*

14. *When Bobby Bonds struck out 189 times in 1970, he broke his own record of 187, established one year earlier in 1969. Mickey Mantle led the American League in strikeouts for five nonconsecutive years. Mickey never struck out more than 126 times a season.*

15. *The minor league player who had assumed the name of a president (Wilson) finally quit after playing only fourteen games. This "Wilson" was our thirty-fourth president, Dwight D. Eisenhower.*

16. *The 1908 Chicago White Sox hit a total of three home runs during the entire season. It is hard to believe, but it is in* The Guinness Book of Records.

17. *Bucky said that*
 he got his wish to be traded to the Yankees
 he got to play in the World Series
 he found his father.
Dent had been brought up by foster parents and had spent years searching for his real father. In 1978 his search was successful.

18. *Early in his career, Reagan worked as an announcer for the Chicago Cubs.*

19. *In a four-year period Reggie Jackson struck out 609 times. Vince DiMaggio led the National League in strikeouts four straight years. In the four-year period Vince's total was 389.*

20. *Walter Johnson has a high school named in his honor in Bethesda, Maryland. The students of Abraham Lincoln Junior High*

School in Lindsay, California, voted to change their school's name to Steve Garvey Junior High School.

21. *The Washington Senators, perennial cellar dwellers, were the butt of: "First in war, first in peace, and last in the American League." (The original saying, about George Washington, is: "First in war, first in peace, and first in the hearts of his country- men.")*

22. *It was the first major league night game.*

23. *The players on the first baseball team wore straw hats, white shirts, and blue full-length trousers. The umpires wore Prince Albert coats and silk hats.*

Top of the Seventh

1. Who holds the record for having reached first base safely the most times during a single season?

2. Who began the practice of giving out with an auctioneer's, "Going, going, gone!" as a home run sailed out of the park?

3. This American League player led the league in batting yet failed to hit one home run during the season. Name him.

4. In 1969 the same player as in the previous question did something most unusual on the base paths. What?

5. What was so unusual about the 1964 American League batting title?

6. Which of these catchers have won batting titles? Mickey Cochrane, Bill Dickey, Yogi Berra, Gabby Hartnett, Roy Campanella, Johnny Bench, or Carlton Fisk?

7. Name eight moving pictures that have a baseball background.

8. Name the men who served the most years as manager.

9. The Atlanta Braves have had many names prior to their present one. What are they?

10. This pitcher has a victory over every club in both leagues. Name him.

11. Why was Brooklyn Dodger Harold Reese called "Pee Wee"?

ANSWERS

1. *Babe Ruth holds the record for having reached first base safely the most times during a single season with a 379 total. The National League's record holder is Lefty O'Doul with a 334 total.*

2. *"Going, going, gone!" originated with Mel Allen, the "Voice of the New York Yankees" for twenty-five years.*

3. *Rod Carew led the league in hitting yet failed to hit one home run during the season.*

4. *In 1969 Rod Carew stole home seven times.*

5. *It was won by a rookie, Tony Oliva.*

6. *None of the catchers named ever won a batting title. Only two catchers in history have won it. Ernie Lombardi twice and Bubbles Hargrave once. (Under present-day rules, Hargrave would not qualify.)*

7. *Some movies with baseball background:*
> **Take Me Out to the Ball Game**, *with Gene Kelly*
> **Elmer the Great**, *with Joe E. Brown*
> **The Stratton Story**, *with James Stewart*
> **The Babe Ruth Story**, *with William Bendix*
> **The Kid from Left Field**, *with Dan Dailey*
> **Rhubarb**, *with Ray Milland*
> **It Happened in Flatbush**, *with Lloyd Nolan*
> **Pride of the Yankees**, *with Gary Cooper*

8. *These men served the most years as managers:*
> *Connie Mack, fifty-three*
> *John McGraw, thirty-four*
> *Bucky Harris, twenty-nine*
> *Bill McKechnie, twenty-five*
> *Casey Stengel, twenty-five*

9. *The Atlanta Braves have had a number of names prior to their present one:*

1876-1890	*Boston Red Stockings, Reds or Red Caps*
	(no relation to the present-day Red Sox)
1891-1906	*Boston Beaneaters*
1907-1910	*Boston Doves*
1911-	*Boston Rustlers*
1912-1935	*Boston Braves*
1936-1940	*Boston Bees*
1941-1952	*Boston Braves*
1953-1965	*Milwaukee Braves*
1966-	*Atlanta Braves*

10. *Rick Wise, pitching today, has a victory over every team in the majors.*

11. *Reese was a marble-shooting champion in his youth; peewees are marbles.*

Seventh Inning Stretch

Stockton, California, believes that it can prove that the poem "Casey at the Bat" was written about their city. The poem first appeared in Ernest L. Thayer's column in the San Francisco *Examiner* on June 3, 1888. The players mentioned in the poem—Cooney, Flynn, Blake, Barrows, and Casey—all played for the Stockton team that year.

The dock area, where the games were played at that time, was called "Mudville."

Stockton once staged a great pageant with Max Baer, one-time world's heavyweight boxing champion, taking the part of Casey.

Roy Campanella once said, "I love this baseball. The day they take that uniform off me, they'll have to rip it off—and when they do, they can bury me." Sad, prophetic words. In mid-career, the great Campy was paralyzed in an automobile crash.

"Joe," said Marilyn, just back from Korea, "you don't know what it's like to have 50,000 people cheering and yelling your name!"

"Yes I do."

Ralph Kiner led the National League in home runs for seven consecutive years, 1946-1952. His wife, Nancy, was a tennis champion. Ralph was quite competitive, and although he only took up tennis when they married, he told Nancy that some day he would beat her. At last the day came when he did, 7-5, 7-5. "And two days later," Ralph tells it, "our first child was born."

One night while Ted Williams was living in Florida, he heard a sound on the roof of his cabin. He made a grab for a loaded baseball bat. He stepped outside and found himself looking into the eyes of a ferocious bobcat. The animal leaped at Ted. The bobcat had no chance against the swing that propelled 521 home runs over the fence.

The late Tom Yawkey, owner of the Boston Red Sox, did not know the extent of his own wealth. One day he was passing a rather attractive office building in New York. He hadn't noticed it before, but now he was interested. He asked one of his officers to see about buying it.

Twenty-four hours later the officer completed his research, and he phoned to say, "Mr. Yawkey, you can't buy that building. You already own it."

The year was 1942. The place, Braves Field, Boston. The Braves were playing the Phils. Paul Waner of the Braves was on third base when Max West hit a ground ball and was thrown out at first base. West was naturally disappointed, and he jogged back to the dugout. As he reached a point just behind the catcher, the Phils' pitcher uncorked a wild throw, which sailed over the catcher's head toward the grandstand. Waner started trotting in from third. West, however, spotting the ball, instinctively grabbed it and tossed it to the Phils' catcher, who put the tag on the surprised Waner. West had made an uncredited assist, putting out his own teammate.

Tom Zachary, who pitched Ruth's sixtieth home run, looked at it as something that had been hung around his neck for over forty years. He said, "I should have thrown the damned ball at his fat head!"

More than ten years after he retired, Ty Cobb was shooting the breeze with Nig Clarke, a crusty catcher. Clarke was

bragging that his hands were so fast umpires would call runners out even though he didn't tag them. "Gosh, Ty, there
must have been at least a dozen times when I missed you and
you were called out. "You cost me twelve runs!" Cobb yelled,
and proceeded to beat him up.

Charley Grimm enjoyed baiting umpires. Approaching the
umpire working behind the plate, he would say, "Sir, you're
supposed to look *through* those glasses, not over them."
    The startled umpire would reply, "I'm not wearing glasses!"
"Oh!" Charlie would say, "I'm sorry. I thought you were."

Paul Waner was a .350 hitter for the Pirates. Pie Traynor, his
manager, thought that Paul was capable of hitting .400. The
only catch was that Paul would have to give up drinking the
hard stuff—an occasional beer would be OK.
    After the first month of semi-abstinence, Paul was batting
only .250. Paul and Pie stopped at a bar. The bartender asked
Paul what he'd have. Paul replied virtuously, "Give me a
beer." Pie turned to the bartender and said, "Like hell! Give
him a shot of whiskey."

Bob Feller, a great fastballer, was on the mound for Cleveland. Lefty Gomez stepped up to the plate in the last inning
and suggested to the umpire that he call the game because of
darkness.
    The ump stared him down. "Play ball," he said.
    Lefty took out a match and lit it.
    "What's the idea," said the ump. "Can't you see Feller?"
    "I sure can," said Lefty. "I just want to be sure Feller can
see *me*!"

Some time during the season, when relief pitcher "Fireman"
Johnny Murphy had put out a number of blazes the opposing
team had lit under Lefty Gomez, someone asked Lefty what he
thought his record would be that year.
    "I'll win twenty games," said Gomez, "—if Murphy's arm
holds out."
    (Murphy was sometimes called "Grandma" because of his
rocking-chair motion as he wound up.)

Rube Waddell and his roommate, Ossie Schreckengost, got along very well except for Waddell's habit of having a snack before he went to sleep. Finally, Schreckengost had a clause inserted in his contract: "Waddell is prohibited from eating crackers in bed." The management went along with it.

One Friday, the Dodgers were flying to a game when the stewardess offered a steak to Gil Hodges, a Catholic. Meat was a forbidden item on Friday in those days. "How high up is this plane?" Gil asked. "About twenty thousand feet," replied the stewardess. Gil shook his head and said, "No, thank you. We're too close to headquarters."

Dizzy Dean bet a friend fifty cents that he would strike out Vince DiMaggio every time he came up during the game. He did this the first three times Vince came to the plate. When Vince came to the plate the last time, he lifted a game-ending foul fly behind the plate. Dizzy shouted to his catcher, Bruce Ogrodowski—"Drop it! Drop it!" Bruce was stunned and dropped it. Dizzy then struck out Vince, winning his fifty-cent bet.

Wilbert Robinson, the Dodger manager, once decided to start a rookie named Oscar Roettger. Writing up the lineup that had to be handed to the umpire before the game, he began, "R-O-T-G..." stopped, and erased it. Tried again, "R-E-T-T..." and finally threw down his pencil. "Aw, the devil! Let Cox stay in right field!"

Brooks Robinson once reminded Stan Musial that he was his boyhood idol. Stan, who was still playing ball at the time, said, "You sure know how to hurt a guy."

Abner Doubleday has been given credit for founding the game of baseball on the word of a long-time resident of Cooperstown, New York, named Abner Graves. Graves stated that he remembered Abner Doubleday laying out a diamond in Cooperstown sixty-eight years previously.

The Baseball Hall of Fame was established in 1936 at Cooperstown, New York. Each year senior writers vote on which players of the preceding twenty years should be enshrined. To be elected, a player must be named on 75 percent of the ballots. Each year a special committee also passes on the admission of old-timers.

It was during the war when a number of servicemen visited the Vatican. Among those who were granted an audience with Pope Pius XII was Ducky Medwick, former St. Louis Cardinal outfielder. The Pope asked each in turn his vocation in civilian life. When it came to Ducky's turn, he said, "Your Holiness, I am Joseph Medwick. I also used to be a Cardinal."

There are many, many stories about Yogi Berra. Some must be apocryphal, and others could be true. It is hard to separate fact and hearsay. Most of them poke fun at Yogi's understanding, whereas, in fact, Yogi was one of the smartest catchers of all time, and a wise baseball manager.

Lawrence Peter Berra was given the name Yogi by his boyhood friends when they compared him to a fakir they had seen in a movie.

Here are two of his so-called malapropisms:
Berra was once given a check made out "To Bearer." Yogi thought they were misspelling his name.

Said Yogi, "Mickey Mantle hits right-handed *and* left-handed. He's naturally amphibious."

One night Toots Shor, the famous restaurateur, introduced Yogi to Ernest Hemingway. "This is the writer," Toots said. "What paper you write for, Ernie?" Yogi asked.

In a radio interview the interviewer mentioned the two hits Yogi had had the previous day. Berra immediately corrected the interviewer and said that it was three hits. The radio man said that he was very sorry; he had read two hits in the box score in the sports section of the newspaper just before the broadcast. The omission of the third hit must have been a typographical error. "Hell, no, it was a clean single to left," Yogi said.

Joe E. Brown, famous actor and avid baseball fan was quite proud of his trophy room. Joe once approached his very good friend Lou Gehrig, asking Lou for his glove when Lou retired. Lou replied that he wished Joe had asked for anything but his glove. Wouldn't Joe settle for Lou's bat or his shoes?

During his last World Series, a gray, thin Lou Gehrig called Joe over to the dugout and personally handed him his glove.

Ty Cobb went into the stands and attacked an abusive heckler. He was placed on suspension. The other Detroit players thought the suspension unfair. They refused to play. It was probably the first players' strike on record.

Detroit was scheduled to play Connie Mack's Athletics. It was a "must play" game for Detroit. If they forfeited the game it would cost the club $5,000. Connie suggested that Detroit hire a group of collegians from St. Joseph's Seminary in Philadelphia for this one game. The collegians, plus one sandlotter, were signed to regular major league contracts.

On the 18th of May, 1912, this motley group pranced on the field to play a regular league game with the world champion Philadelphia Athletics. Joe Travers from St. Joseph's pitched for the Tigers. He allowed twenty-four runs, which is still the record for a single game. Detroit lost 24 to 2. The collegians committed nine errors. Joe Travers, whose name is in the record books, later became a priest.

Wilbert Robinson had been a catcher in the majors for many years. Weighing about 300 pounds, he was now managing Brooklyn. In the spring of 1917, just before an exhibition game at Fort Lauderdale, Florida, he said that he would catch a baseball dropped from an aeroplane. Down it came, hitting Robbie on the chest and felling him to the ground. Everybody thought that he was dead. But someone had substituted a grapefruit filled with catsup for the ball. No one found out who the culprit or joker was, but one player was traded on circumstantial evidence. Casey Stengel went to the Pirates.

The suspicion was probably justified. It was Stengel, remember, who once tipped his hat during a game—and a pigeon flew out!

When the Dodgers first moved into the Coliseum, Duke Snider bet that he could become the first man to throw a baseball out of the place. His first throw fell nineteen rows short of the top. He tried a second time and immediately strained his valuable throwing arm. Alston benched him and fined him $275.

"When you unwrap one, it tells you how good it is." (Catfish Hunter, talking about the candy bar named for Yankee teammate Reggie Jackson.)

Paul Waner often sipped from a Coke bottle while in the dugout.

One time, the innocent batboy took a drink from Paul's Coke bottle and woke up the next morning with a hangover.

Once asked to what he owed his success, Lefty Gomez replied, "Clean living—and a fast outfield."

"El Goofo" also complained in the later years of his career that "I'm throwing the ball just as hard as ever, but it's not getting to the plate as fast!"

A rabid Boston rooter was given this hypothetical situation: "If a cabin containing your wife and Ted Williams started toppling over a fifteen-thousand-foot cliff, and you had a choice of saving just one of them, which would you choose?" The rooter answered angrily. "Are you out of your mind? My wife can't hit."

In early 1973 Nolan Ryan pitched a no-hitter against Kansas City. Two months later he was going against the Detroit Tigers. Ryan was overpowering. He fanned twelve of the first fourteen batters he faced. In the fifth inning Norm Cash of Detroit walked up to the plate with a Ping-Pong paddle. The umpire tossed the paddle away. In the ninth Cash came up swinging a piano leg. The ump should have given Cash the heave-ho, but he didn't. Nolan went on to his second no-hitter of the season.

In 1950 Eddie Montague (former major leaguer) was asked by the New York Giants to look at a first baseman in one of the teams in the Negro Leagues.

At this game Eddie saw a player who set his mind a-whirling. He called New York and told them to forget the first baseman, but that he had seen a player who was out of this world. He insisted that the Giants sign him right now. They did just that. So, to Eddie Montague goes the honor of finding the incomparable Willie Mays, while looking for a first baseman.

Master showman Bill Veeck once livened up a game for his St. Louis fans by putting a midget, Eddie Gaedel, in the Browns' batting order. Before the game he asked Eddie what he knew about baseball. Eddie replied, "I know you're supposed to hit the white ball with the bat and then you run somewhere." When Bill heard this, he flipped. "Now listen," he said "I'm going to be up on the roof with a high-powered rifle watching every move you make. You just stand there and take four pitches. If you so much as look as if you're going to swing at the ball, I'll shoot you dead!"

So, Eddie walked up to the plate, and Detroit pitcher, Bob Cain, threw him four straight balls. Cain couldn't stop laughing.

The year was 1908. Jack Norworth was riding an elevated train in New York City. The car in which he was riding carried an ad for the New York Giants baseball game. Sitting there, Norworth had an inspiration. He started writing and before he had finished his half-hour ride had completed the words to the song, *Take Me Out to the Ball Game*.

Norworth had never seen a major league game; in fact, the first one that he saw was in Brooklyn thirty-four years later.

Albert von Tilzer, who composed the music, did not see his first major league game until twenty years later.

Norworth also wrote the classic song, *Shine on Harvest Moon*.

Bottom of the Seventh

1. Identify these players from their nicknames:
   "The Meal Ticket"
   "The Mechanical Man"
   "Twinkletoes"
   "The Fordham Flash"

2. Who wore the number 1/8 on his uniform?

3. How many of the following baseball immortals can you give uniform numbers for?

   Leo Durocher   Bob Feller
   Joe DiMaggio   Willie Mays
   Carl Yastrzemski   Casey Stengel
   Whitey Ford   Lou Gehrig and Mel Ott
   Bobby Thomson   Mickey Mantle
   Sandy Koufax   Carl Hubbell
   Hank Aaron and Willie McCovey   Roberto Clemente
   Babe Ruth   Satchel Paige
   Stan Musial   Jackie Robinson
   Ted Williams   Don Drysdale

4. What is the story of the origin of the Yankees' pin-striped uniforms?

5. Who was baseball's youngest major league player?

6. During regular play this National Leaguer was at bat twenty times and hit ten home runs. Who was he?

7. Did it always take four balls to get a base on balls?

8. In one game George Sisler fielded the ball and tossed it lightly to first base. Much to his surprise, he found that the pitcher wasn't covering. Who caught the ball?

9. This Hall of Famer once faced a fire-balling pitcher with two strikes on him. The pitcher reared back and threw his hardest fast ball—and the batter caught it in his bare hand. The umpire called him out, but the pitcher was so upset he walked the next five batters, losing the game. Who was the hitter?

10. How much time does a pitcher have to deliver the ball after receiving it?

11. What odd home run record does Maury Wills hold?

12. Now we call them "innings." What were they originally called? What were runs originally called?

ANSWERS

1. *"The Mealticket"*—Carl Hubbell
   "The Mechanical Man"—Charley Gehringer
   "Twinkletoes"—George Selkirk
   "The Fordham Flash"—Frankie Frisch

2. *Eddie Gaedel, Bill Veeck's midget.*

3. Leo Durocher, **2**
   Joe DiMaggio, **5**
   Carl Yastrzemski, **8**
   Whitey Ford, **16**
   Bobby Thomson, **23**
   Sandy Koufax, **32**
   Hank Aaron and Willie
   McCovey, **44**
   Babe Ruth, **3**
   Stan Musial, **6**
   Ted Williams, **9**

   Bob Feller, **19**
   Willie Mays, **24**
   Casey Stengel, **37**
   Lou Gehrig and Mel
   Ott, **4**
   Mickey Mantle, **7**
   Carl Hubbell, **11**
   Roberto Clemente, **21**
   Satchel Paige, **29**
   Jackie Robinson, **42**
   Don Drysdale, **53**

4. *It has been said that the Yankees wear pin-striped uniforms because owner Jake Ruppert thought that Babe Ruth looked too fat in his white uniform. Pin stripes are supposed to be slimming, and it's been pin stripes for the New York team ever since. (I cannot attest to the authenticity of this, but it makes a good story.)*

5. *Joe Nuxhall, who pitched for Cincinnati in 1944 at the age of fifteen years, ten months and eleven days.*

6. *Frank Howard.*

7. *No. In 1879 it took a call of nine balls to get a base on balls. In 1880 it was reduced to eight, in 1881 to seven, in 1884 to six, in 1885 to seven, in 1887 to five, and in 1889 the four-ball walk was instituted.*

8. *Sisler himself made it to first in time to catch his own throw!*

9. *Honus Wagner*

10. *Twenty seconds if there is anyone on base; no specified limit if bases are empty.*

11. *In the same game Wills hit a home run batting left-handed and another batting right-handed.*

12. *Innings were originally called "hands," runs were "aces."*

Eighth Inning

1. The first no-hitter pitched in the National League was hurled by Joe Borden in 1876. Later the same year he had a different position on the club. What was it?

2. This was a question that the great Honus Wagner liked to stop his friends with: How could a player hit a game-winning home run with bases loaded and yet have not one man touch home plate?

3. The Dodgers installed a new pitching machine and gave it a name. What did they call it?

4. These two batters share the National League record of 254 hits in a single season. Name them.

5. This player pitched in the 1920 World Series. His son pitched in the 1946 World Series. Name this father and son duo.

6. Who was the toughest pitcher to strike out? He once went through an entire season without striking out once. He came to bat ninety-four times.

7. There have been many rhubarbs among players, umpire, etc., but I believe this one tops them all. In May 1894 John McGraw, then with the Baltimore Orioles, got into a fight with the Boston third baseman. What did it lead to?

8. On May 26, 1959, a pitcher for the Pittsburgh Pirates performed one of the gretest feats in baseball history, but the story has a sad ending. Who was the pitcher, what did he do, and what happened?

9. Webster's *American Biographies* says, "Perhaps his most memorable achievement as a Dodger came in his last game at Ebbets Field when he gave Casey Stengel a hot-

foot. Just who was it who gave Old Case the hotfoot? Hint: you would ordinarily not expect to have seen him at a ball park.

10. In 1935, 1936, and 1937 players whose last names begin with the letter "G" won the M.V.P. Award in the American League. Name them.

11. This president of the United States once owned a baseball club in Ohio. He could keep a box score that would match that of any professional. On the edges of his score card, he noted the bets he had made with the members of his Cabinet. Name this president.

12. Casey Stengel managed the Yankees through 574 World Series innings. How many Series does this represent?

13. Joe McCarthy managed the Cubs, Yankees, and the Red Sox. What was his nickname?

14. It is the 1939 World Series; tenth inning, the pitcher uncorks a wild pitch. The catcher blocks it with his body, then can't find it even though the ball is only three feet from him. Two runs score in all the confusion. Name the two teams involved and the unfortunate catcher.

15. In 1968 Detroit's second baseman came to bat 570 times. His name is Dick McAuliffe. What did McAuliffe avoid doing in all 570 times at bat?

16. It is October 2, 1920; two National League teams are playing a triple-header—three games in one day. How come?

17. Three men have managed pennant winners in both the American and National Leagues. Name them.

18. Columnist Jim Murray said this regarding a certain baseball player. Quote. "Pound for pound he may be the best ever to play the game." To whom was he referring?

19. How are official scorers chosen?

20. The name Thayer bobs up twice in baseball history. Ernest Thayer who wrote "Casey at the Bat." F. W. Thayer, a student at Harvard, invented something. What?

21. When Yankee Stadium opened in 1923, a man who was to run unsuccessfully for president tossed out the first ball. Name him.

22. From what are the covers of baseballs made?

23. Five minutes before a game the umpire receives each team's batting order in duplicate. What does he do with them?

ANSWERS

1. *After Joe Borden pitched the National League's first no-hitter, he lost his effectiveness and ended up the same year as the team's groundskeeper.*

2. *The answer? It was a woman's team.*

3. *As an inspiration for their hitters, the Dodgers named their pitching machine "Warren Spahn."*

4. *The National League record of 254 is shared by Bill Terry and Lefty O'Doul. The record for most hits in a single season, 257, is held by George Sisler.*

5. *Jim Bagby and his son, Jim Junior, each pitched in a World Series. Jim Senior pitched for Cleveland in the 1920 Series, and Jim Junior took the mound for the Red Sox in 1946.*

6. *Johnny Sain of the Boston Braves. His record "no-strikeout" year—at bat, that is—was 1946.*

7. *Before long the players on both teams were fighting. Then it spread to the audience. The spectators set fire to the bleachers. Soon the entire ball park was burned to the ground, along with 170 other nearby buildings.*

8. *Harvey Haddix of the Pirates pitched a perfect game for twelve innings, three more than required for credit for a perfect major league game. Consider that there had never been a perfect game in the National League since 1880.*

In the thirteenth inning Don Hoak made a throwing error, allowing the Braves' Felix Mantilla to reach first base. Eddie Matthews sacrificed Mantilla to second. Hank Aaron was walked intentionally to load the bases. Joe Adcock doubled, scoring Mantilla and giving the Braves a 1-0 victory over Haddix.

(Adcock actually hit a pitch into the center field stands for what should have been a home run. But Aaron thought that the ball was still in the park, and he headed for the dugout. Adcock was given a double and then ruled out for passing Aaron on the base path, but Mantilla's run had scored and the game was lost for Haddix.)

9. *Emmett Kelly, the world-renowned clown. He was employed by the team's management to entertain the fans before the game.*

10. *In 1935, '36, and '37 players whose last names began with the letter "G" won the M.V.P. Award.*
> *1935: Hank Greenberg*
> *1936: Lou Gehrig*
> *1937: Charley Gehringer*

11. *President Warren Harding once owned a baseball team.*

12. *Ten series, of which his Yankees won seven.*

13. *Joe McCarthy's nickname was "Marse Joe," given him by Chicago sportswriter Harry Neky.*

14. *In the 1939 World Series between the Yankees and Cincinnati, the Cincy pitcher uncorked a wild pitch. The catcher, Ernie Lombardi, blocked the ball. It was practically in front of him, yet he couldn't find it as two runs swept across the plate. The Yankees won the Series in four games. Ernie is the only catcher, under modern rules to win a batting championship. When Hargrave won the batting title in 1926, the only rule was that a player had to appear in at least 100 games to be eligible. In 1945 the rule was changed to 400 times. Now it is 502 times, probably because of the 162-game schedule.*

15. *In 1968 Detroit second baseman Dick McAuliffe came to bat 570 times without hitting into a double play.*

16. *Pittsburgh and Cincinnati played the triple-header. It was the next-to-the-last day of the season. Pittsburgh had a chance to finish third, ahead of Cincinnati. Pittsburgh, needing a sweep of the three games (one a make-up game), lost the first two. They won the third game, which was called at the end of the sixth inning since the outcome was academic.*

17. *Joe McCarthy, Yogi Berra, and Alvin Dark.*

18. *Syndicated columnist Jimmy Murray said that "Pound for pound Joe Morgan may be the best ever to play the game." Morgan is the Cincinnati Reds' smallest player: 5 foot 7 inches tall, 165 pounds. He was voted the National League's M.V.P. twice in a row, in 1975 and 1976.*

19. *Official scorers are generally baseball writers who are assigned to a particular club or clubs during the regular season.*

They are chosen by members of the local chapter of the Baseball Writers Association of America. They get in the neighborhood of $70 for scoring each game.

20. *The catcher's mask.*

21. *When Yankee Stadium was opened in 1923, the first ball was tossed out by Al Smith, governor of New York and later a candidate for the presidency.*

22. *Baseballs are called "horsehides" even though the covering is actually made of cowhide.*

23. *He keeps one copy and gives the other to the opposing manager.*

Ninth Inning

1. Frankie Frisch played second base for Fordham University and later became a Cardinal. A few years earlier, Fordham had a second-string second baseman who also became a Cardinal. What was his name.

2. Houston's Astrodome is rainproof, yet a game was once called because of rain. The date was June 15, 1976. How come?

3. On the night of August 25, 1930, fighter Frankie Campbell was knocked out by Max Baer and died from the blow. What was Campbell's indirect connection with the game of baseball?

4. Why should one question stolen base records established between 1886 and 1898?

5. What have Tom Seaver, Fred Lynn, Dave Kingman, Bill Lee, and Jim Barr in common?

6. Umpire Bill Guthrie once threw Babe Ruth out of a game and told him to "take the batboy with you!" Was he really evicting the batboy?

7. When Babe Ruth hit his sixty home runs, two of them came with the bases loaded. How many bases-loaded home runs did Roger Maris hit in his record-breaking sixty-one homer season?

8. Name the only professional baseball player to address Congress. What was the occasion?

9. All of the following happened in a single World Series game.

A home run with the bases loaded.

The first home run by a pitcher in a World Series game.

The first unassisted triple play in a World Series.

The batter who had hit into the triple play hit into a double play the next time up. In two at-bats he accounted for five outs.

Name the teams. When did it happen?

10. It is the last of the ninth inning; Johnny VanderMeer has the bases loaded with two outs. He needs one more out to complete his double no-hitter. Name the player he faced.

11. In 1917 Johnny Evers played for the Phils and batted .231. In 1929 he played second base for the Boston Braves. Guess how many hits Hall of Famer Evers got in those twelve years.

12. It is the fourth game of the 1957 World Series between the New York Yankees and the Milwaukee Braves. Nippy Jones of the Braves is at bat. Tommy Byrne of the Yankees throws his first pitch to Jones. Jones runs to first base but is called back by the umpire. Jones claims that he had been hit on the foot. The umpire disagrees. Jones keeps arguing and finally wins his point. How did Jones convince the umpire that he had been hit?

13. The number 97 has a special significance to both Don Larsen and Sandy Koufax. How come?

14. How many members of the White Sox were indicted for throwing the 1919 World Series? Were they found guilty?

15. Dan Bankhead was the first black pitcher in the majors. The year was 1947. In his first game Dan did something he was never to repeat in the fifty-two games he pitched during his career. What?

16. What record does Jim Gentile share with Ernie Banks?

17. He was known as "Home Run" Baker. He led the American League in homers three years in a row; 1911, 1912, and 1913. What is the highest number of home runs he ever hit in a single season?

18. One old-time player refused to pitch on Sunday. There was a modern-day pitcher who refused to pitch a World Series game for religious reasons. Who were these players? Why did the modern pitcher balk at working in what Damon Runyon characters called "The Serious"?

19. In greyhound racing the dogs chase a mechanical rabbit. Not too long ago one of our baseball teams featured a mechanical rabbit. Name this team.

20. There's a curious insurance statistic that should be a consolation for a player with a low lifetime batting average. What is it?

21. The actuaries also find that a player who plays a particular position on a baseball team lives longer than those at the other eight positions. Name the position.

22. Why do most ball players chew either gum or tobacco?

23. In his last at-bat before his death in an airplane crash, Roberto Clemente had hit a magic number. Just what was it?

24. In 1961 this National League club went through the entire season without a manager. Name this team.

ANSWERS

1. *The Fordham substitute second baseman who later became a Cardinal was Francis Cardinal Spellman.*

2. *Houston's Astrodome is impervious to rain, yet in June 1976 a game was called on account of rain. There was a torrential rainstorm in Houston. It rained about 7½ inches in three hours. Fans were unable to get to the dome.*

3. *Fighter Frankie Campbell was knocked out by Max Baer and died. Frankie was the brother of Dolf Camilli, major league baseball player.*

4. *A runner would be given a stolen base merely by advancing an extra base on a hit. For example, he would get two stolen bases on a triple.*

5. *They all went to the University of Southern California, the college that has contributed more players to the major leagues than any other.*

6. *No. He was referring to the Yankee manager, Miller Huggins, who was a very small man—physically.*
One ball player who ended up in the Hall of Fame was so small that on first seeing him, the owner of the club ordered the manager to "get that batboy out of there!" It was Wee Willie Keeler, who was 5 feet, 3 inches tall. Keeler holds the record of 199 singles in a season and hit in forty-four straight games—a record that stood for a long time before Joe DiMaggio surpassed it.
Keeler's recipe for success at bat was to "Hit 'em where they ain't."

7. *When Babe Ruth hit his sixty home runs, two of them came with the bases loaded. In his record sixty-one Maris had none with the bags loaded.*

8. *Only one professional baseball player has addressed Congress, Hank Aaron.*

9. *The fifth game of the 1920 World Series between Brooklyn and Cleveland produced four records: the first homer by a pitcher, Jim Bagby; a homer with the bases loaded; an unassisted triple play; and a batter accounting for five outs in only two times at bat.*

10. *The last man Johnny VanderMeer faced to complete his double no-hitter was Leo Durocher. Durocher, a brilliant fielder, was a minor threat at bat—he was known as "the all-American out." But any hitter can be dangerous at times.*

11. *Johnny Evers last played as a regular in 1917. In 1922, as a coach for the Chicago White Sox, he batted in one game, with no hits. In 1929, as the Boston Braves manager, he came up once with the same result. So, in a span of twelve years, he made no hits. Ty Cobb didn't worry a bit.*

12. *In the 1957 World Series between the Yanks and Milwaukee, Nippy Jones claimed that he had been hit by Tommy Byrne's pitch. The umpire said "no," then reversed his decision after looking at a big black splotch on the ball. Jones was wearing a pair of newly polished shoes.*

13. *It took Don Larsen exactly ninety-seven pitches to throw his perfect game. Sandy Koufax struck out ten or more batters in a game ninety-seven times.*

14. *Eight members of the White Sox were indicted for throwing the 1919 World Series. They were acquitted but were banished from baseball forever by the Commissioner of Baseball.*

15. *Dan Bankhead, first black pitcher in the majors, hit a home run his first time at bat in the "Bigs." It was his last major league home run.*

16. *Ernie Banks and Jim Gentile share the record of hitting five home runs with the bases loaded in a single season. Gentile did it in 1961, Banks in 1955.*

17. *Twelve. John Franklin Baker, known as "Home Run Baker," played third base for Connie Mack's $100,000 infield. This infield consisted of Stuffy McInnis, Eddie Collins, and Jack Barry.*

18. *Christy Mathewson would not play on Sunday, and Sandy Koufax refused to pitch a World Series game because it was Yom Kippur.*

19. *The Oakland A's. One of Charley Finley's innovations was a mechanical rabbit. This rabbit would come out of the ground with additional baseballs.*

20. *Insurance statisticians claim that ball players with low lifetime batting averages tend to live longer than players with high lifetime batting averages. Perhaps it's the tension.*

21. *Third base.*

22. *The reason most players chew tobacco or gum is to keep from drinking too much water.*

23. *In more than one hundred years of major league baseball, fourteen batters have made 3,000 or more hits during their careers. (This figure includes Lou Brock, who reached the magic number while this book was in preparation.) For Roberto Clemente, however, number 3,000 was his last hit.*

Roberto Clemente ranks high among the finest gentlemen and baseball players of all time.

After his team had won the 1971 World Series, he was asked to say a few words on television. He, in turn, asked to say a few words to his parents. In deep, genuine humility he said in Spanish, "On this, the proudest moment of my life, I ask your blessing."

24. *The Cubs did not have a manager during the 1961 season. Owner Phil Wrigley decided to try a rotating staff of head coaches to run the team.*

Extra Inning:
The Tie Breaker

1. What do these catcher's signals mean:
   One finger in the palm of the glove?
   Two fingers in the palm of the glove?

2. When a player is "shooting stingers," he is not throwing the ball hard or hitting screaming line drives. What is he doing?

3. This somewhat earthy nickname for a catcher—any catcher—isn't heard on the airwaves, but the players use it. What is it?

4. A *homer* is, of course, a home run— a *round tripper*, a four-base hit. But the word "homer" has another, pejorative meaning. What is it?

5. What do a player's teammates say when they notice his hair is getting thin on top?

6. Pity the poor player with *bad wheels*. A "Day" for him, with the customary presentation of a new automobile, won't help much on the field. What is the ball player's meaning of *bad wheels*?

7. When they call a player a *muffin*, they're not buttering him up! Great hitter Ralph Kiner was a muffin. What does it mean?

8. Why, in an argument over an umpire's call, might an incensed player mutter that the arbiter is a "Mr. Magoo"?

9. Complimentary tickets are called "Annie Oakleys" because they sometimes have so many holes punched in them that the legendary markswoman might have been shooting at them. What incident in a ball game is called an *Annie Oakley* as well?

10. What does a player mean when he tells another, during a game, to "take the blood off it"?

11. What is a *wounded duck?*

12. What is a *lollipop?*

13. What is a *tickey?*

14. "He talks big, but he doesn't have guts." What is he?

15. He couldn't talk so big if he had a *hot pipe*. Why?

16. Pop music stars have groupies. What is the term for women who follow their favorite baseball player from city to city?

ANSWERS

1. *Every team has its own signals between catcher and pitcher. But one finger calls for a fast ball, two for a curve.*

2. *He's ogling an attractive woman in the stands.*

3. *A* hind snatcher.

4. *An umpire who is accused of favoring the home team is referred to, insultingly, as a homer.*

5. *They tell him he has* bad moss.

6. Bad wheels, *in baseball parlance, are troublesome legs, the curse of a ball player's (relative) old age.*

7. *A muffin is a player who is a good hitter, but whose fielding performance leaves something to be desired.*

8. *Mr. Magoo is the animated cartoon character who is nearsighted to the point of blindness. The worst insult to an umpire is to imply that he can't see.*

9. *A base on balls is a free pass to first—an Annie Oakley.*

10. *He is implying that the other player's just-earned hit was a lucky one.*

11. *A short fly to the outfield; like a wounded duck, it can't go very far.*

12. *Any ball thrown with less than normal speed, by any player.*

13. *A batted ball caught immediately by the catcher.*

14. *He's an* alligator mouth.

15. *A* hot pipe, *in player parlance, is a sore throat.*

16. Baseball Annies.

The Bull Pen

Visitors'
Home Team

Visitors' Bull Pen

1. It is June 11, 1938; Johnny VanderMeer of the Reds pitched his second successive no-hitter. This game was pitched at old Ebbets Field in Brooklyn. What else was notable about that game?

2. Name the first black pitcher to win a World Series game.

3. Only one pitcher has pitched a no-hitter on opening day. Name him.

4. On the afternoon of August 16, 1920, a star shortstop was struck by a pitched ball and became the only player in history to be killed in a major league game. Name the pitcher who threw the ball and the shortstop who met such a tragic end.

5. In 1972 Joe Horlen, Vida Blue, Catfish Hunter, and Ken Holtzman all pitched for the Oakland A's in the World Series. What did these four pitchers have in common?

6. There have been excellent hitting pitchers—for example, Babe Ruth and Warren Spahn. This pitcher, in one day, put on a spectacular display of hitting. Name the pitcher, and what did he do?

7. Walter Johnson started the baseball season twelve times. What celebrated figure started the season eight times? You know of him.

8. On Admission Day, 1965, the Cubs were playing the Dodgers in Los Angeles. Charles Hendley, the Cubs pitcher, pitched a superb game, giving the Dodgers one run and only one hit. How many runs and hits did his team get for him?

9. Legendary Walter Johnson lost twenty games in 1916. How many did he win?

10. What did Lefty Gomez, one of baseball's great pitchers and great wits, say about being talented at his sport?

11. Yankee Hall of Famer Red Ruffing originally pitched for the Boston Red Sox. With that team he won a total of thirty-nine games while losing how many?

12. Who holds the National League record for most career home runs hit by a pitcher?

13. You can't place much stock in some of the pitching records made prior to 1890—but here is one that is interesting. Charles ("Old Hoss") Radbourn won more games in a single season than any man in history. The year was 1884. How many?

14. How can a team's players have exactly the same batting averages after a game as it did before the game? There is no gimmick, such as called on account of rain, postponed, etc. This actually happened. A regular nine-inning game was played. There was a winner and a loser, yet the players on one of the teams had exactly the same averages after the game as they had before the game was played. Explain.

15. Christy Mathewson was known for his fadeaway pitch. Today that pitch has another name. What do we call the "fadeaway" today?

16. What is the longest game, in innings, in major league history? What is the longest in terms of time?

17. When this ball player died, a Pittsburgh sportswriter named McGeenan wrote, "There died at Saranac the best loved of all baseball players and the most popular of all American athletes of all time." Name this beloved athlete. (He was not a Pirate.)

18. When Don Larsen pitched his perfect game in the World Series, who was the last man he faced? How did he get him out?

19. Nowadays a person can't buy his way out of the service, but once it was perfectly legal to do so. Jay bought his way out. You probably know Jay by a different name. Name him.

20. In 1906 and 1907 Henry and Christy Mathewson pitched for the New York Giants and established the major league record for wins by brothers. How many did each brother win?

21. It was Mother's Day. She was in the stands to see her son pitch, when an opposing batter's foul ball hit her in the head, knocking her unconscious. At the hospital a grief-stricken son said he was going to give up baseball; but a very understanding mother, now recovered, forbade it. This pitcher went on to an outstanding career in the game. Who was the injured woman's son?

22. A no-hitter is an unusual event, but try to imagine *two* no-hit, no-run games between the same two teams within an eighteen-hour period. When did it happen? Who were the pitchers? What were the teams?

23. A well-known pitcher threw the "Eephus ball," Name him.

24. A manufacturer of unbreakable glass wanted to demonstrate the toughness of the glass, so he asked this famous pitcher to throw his fast ball against the glass. The pitcher let one fly and the ball went clean through the glass. Who was this pitcher?

25. This Boston Celtics basketball player also pitched for the Boston Red Sox and the Boston Braves. Name him.

26. What pitcher holds the record for having hit the most batters?

27. In 1973 this player pitched nine innings for the San Francisco Giants. He also led the team with twenty-six home runs. Name him.

In 1965 this player did a bit of pitching for the Giants and was traded. The following year he led the National League in hitting with a .342 average. Name him.

28. Who was the only pitcher in modern times to pitch a no-hitter in his first major league start? It was in 1953. Where did he go from there?

29. This pitcher in 1972 accomplished the incredible feat of winning twenty-seven games with a last-place club. He also led the league in wins, strikeouts, completed games, earned runs, and innings pitched. Can you name this outstanding pitcher?

30. Name the pitcher who married actor Richard Widmark's daughter.

31. This World Series went seven games. One pitcher appeared in each game as a pitcher. This had never been done before. Name him.

32. Name the last pitcher for the Athletics to work an entire World Series game.

ANSWERS

1. *Johnny VanderMeer's second successive no-hitter was pitched at Ebbets Field in the first night game ever played in Brooklyn.*

2. *Dodger pitcher Joe Black was the first black to win a World Series game, against the Yankees in 1952.*

3. *Bob Feller is the only pitcher to throw a no-hitter on opening day. It was his Cleveland team versus the White Sox at Chicago's Comiskey Park, in 1940.*

4. *On his last day in baseball, August 16, 1920, Ray Chapman was killed by a ball thrown by pitcher Carl Mays of the New York Yankees. Chapman had compiled a strange box score. He batted in second place in Cleveland's lineup. He had come to bat twice. He had made two hits, each a two bagger. He had stolen two bases. He scored two runs. He had two putouts, two assists, and had made two errors. But May's fatal pitch was the first one to Chapman in the fifth inning.*

5. *Joe Horlen, Vida Blue, Catfish Hunter, and Ken Holtzman, all pitching for the A's in the 1972 World Series, had all pitched no-hitters. Hunter's was a perfect game.*

6. *Batting for the Atlanta Braves was the pitcher, Tony Cloninger. He was facing San Francisco Giants pitcher Bob Priddy. The bases were loaded. In a matter of seconds they were unloaded. Tony had smashed a bases-clearing home run. Later in the game he faced Ray Sadecki. The situation was the same. The bases were loaded once again. F.O.B.—Full of Braves. Tony smashed the ball over the fence. It was habit forming. Later in the game he singled in another run. He had established a record for a pitcher—nine runs batted in in a single game. Aside from being a pitcher, Cloninger is the only man in National League history to hit two home runs with the bases loaded in the same game. It has been done a number of times in the American League.*

7. *Walter Johnson started the season twelve times, and President Franklin Delano Roosevelt, by tossing out the first ball, started it eight times.*

8. *None. In that same meeting, the Dodgers' Sandy Koufax pitched a perfect game against the Cubs. A record was established; only one man reached first base during the entire game.*

9. *In 1916 Walter Johnson lost twenty games while winning twenty-five.*

10. *Lefty Gomez said, "I'd rather be lucky than good."*

11. *Ninety-six (which probably explains his move to the Yankees).*

12. *Warren Spahn, with thirty-five. Wes Ferrell is the American League and major league record holder, with thirty-seven. Spahn and Johnny Sain were the mainstays of the Boston Braves in 1948, the year they won the pennant, which gave rise to the Boston fans' precept, "Spahn and Sain, and pray for rain."*

13. *"Old Hoss" Radbourn won sixty games in one season. The previous year he had won only forty-four.*

14. *Bob Feller's no-hit, no-run game on opening day left all averages of the White Sox exactly as they were at the beginning of the game. The Chicago players went into the game with 0-0-0 averages, not having played in the season yet, and did nothing to change them. The final score was 1-0. The game was played in Chicago on April 16, 1940.*

15. *Christy Mathewson's famous "fadeaway pitch" is our present day "screwball," a reverse curve.*

16. *The longest game in major league history took place in Boston, May 1, 1920. The game went twenty-six innings. Neither team won inasmuch as it ended in a one-all tie. Joe Oeschger pitched for the Boston Braves while Leon Cadore chucked for the Dodgers. The game didn't last too long in time, consuming only three hours and fifty-minutes. The tie was replayed in June, with Boston winning, 4-2.*
The longest game on record, in point of time, took seven hours and twenty-three minutes and was played by the New York Mets and the San Francisco Giants on May 31, 1964, in New York. The Giants won in twenty-three innings, 8-6.

17. *Christy Mathewson, who died of tuberculosis. His plaque in the Baseball Hall of Fame reads, "Matty was the master of them all." He pitched for the Giants from 1900 to 1916.*

18. *The last player to face Don Larsen in his perfect game was Dale Mitchell. The count was two strikes and one ball. Mitchell took the next pitch and umpire Babe Pinelli called a third strike to end the game.*

19. *Strange as it may seem, a person could buy his way out of the armed services. Dizzy Dean did just that. It was in the 1920s, when, of course, the nation was at peace.*

20. *Christy won 373, which was the record number; brother Henry won none. The joint record has been broken by Gaylord and Jim Perry, who hold it now.*

21. *If Bob Feller's mother had agreed with him, baseball would have lost one of its all-time greats.*

22. *The date was September 17, 1968. Giant pitcher Gaylord Perry no-hit the St. Louis Cards. Less than eighteen hours later, St. Louis pitcher Ray Washburn returned the compliment. It had never been done before.*

23. *Rip Sewell threw the ball that was called the "Eephus pitch." Rip pitched for the Pirates from 1938 through 1949. His won-and-lost record was 143-97.*

24. *Lefty Grove was noted for his fast ball. If anyone could throw a ball through a pane of "unbreakable" glass, Lefty was the man to do it.*

25. *Gene Conley pitched in the majors from 1952 through 1963. His major league record was ninety-one won and ninety-six lost. Gene was a basketball star for the Boston Celtics, playing with the Boston cagers when baseball was not in season. He was with the team for four winters, three of which were championship years for the Celtics.*

26. *Hall of Famer Walter Johnson holds many pitching records, but I don't believe he was particularly proud of this one—hitting 206 batters during his major league career. Johnson's nickname was "The Big Train" because his fast ball reminded hitters of "The Limited" thundering in.*

27. *In 1973 Dave Kingman pitched for the San Francisco Giants. He also led them in hitting home runs.*
Matty Alou pitched in one game for the Giants—a "laugher" when the San Franciscans were far behind in late innings. Matty was traded to the Pirates in 1965. In 1966 he led the National League in hitting with a .342 average.

28. *Alva "Bobo" Holloman, after starting his first major league game for the St. Louis Browns in 1953, in which he threw a no-hitter, racked up a 3-7 won-lost record. He was optioned to Toronto and never returned to the majors. His first start, in which he threw his no-hitter, was his only complete game in the majors.*

29. *Steve Carlton's feat of winning twenty-seven games in 1972 with a last-place club, the Philadelphia Phillies, earned him the Cy Young Award. This is the only time a pitcher for a cellar team has won the award.*

Steve shares the nine-inning-game strikeout record of nineteen with Tom Seaver and Nolan Ryan.

30. *Sandy Koufax married the daughter of Richard Widmark.*

31. *Darold Knowles, relief pitcher for the Oakland A's in the 1973 World Series against the Mets, appeared in all seven games.*

32. *The last pitcher for the Athletics (then in Philadelphia) to pitch a complete World Series game was Lefty Grove in 1931. Though the Oakland A's won the World Series three consecutive times, no pitcher went the distance. In the last two Series Rollie Fingers appeared twelve times in all.*

Home Team Bull Pen

1. What Hall of Fame pitcher was named for the twenty-second and twenty-fourth president of the United States?

2. This pitcher retired more consecutive batters than any pitcher in history.

3. Christy Mathewson's nickname was "Big Six." Just how did Christy acquire this colorful name?

4. How do the Montreal announcers refer to a pitcher, besides as "pitcher"?

5. He is called the "Unknown Man of Baseball." To whom am I referring?

6. Randy Jones and Christy Mathewson share a remarkable record. Just what is this record?

7. Who holds the record for having pitched the most one-hitters?

8. Bob Feller was sworn into the Navy by another champion. Who?

9. These three pitchers, Al Downing, Tracy Stallard, and Tom Zachary, threw record-making home runs. Identify each.

10. What differentiated the pitchers prior to 1884 from those playing since?

11. Name the youngest player ever elected to the Baseball Hall of Fame.

12. A famous pitcher had the nickname "Mose." Name him.

13. What is Tom Seaver's first name? As you can guess, it is not Tom.

14. Every baseball fan should know the name of the pitcher who struck out more batters in one baseball game than any other pitcher in history. It happened in 1962. Just how many batters did Tom strike out?

15. Pitcher Candy Cummings is in baseball's Hall of Fame, not for any remarkable pitching feats but because of an accomplishment that has affected every baseball game since. What did the "Candyman" do?

16. A trick question: How can a pitcher throw a ball in a straight line, have it come to a full stop, and have it return to his own hand?

17. This pitcher, on just about the hottest day of the year, built a camp fire in front of the dugout. Who was it?

18. The spitball was outlawed in 1920. When it was outlawed, each team was permitted to designate two pitchers who were then throwing the spitter to continue using it until the end of their careers. The question is this: Who was the last pitcher to throw the spitter (officially, that is)? Also, when was the last time that it was thrown?

19. In the 1905 World Series this pitcher started three games, pitching three shutouts. This same pitcher won twenty-three games in 1912, none of which were shutouts. Name him.

20. What does pitching ace Don Gullett say was the biggest thrill of his athletic career?

21. Only once in the history of baseball have four pitchers combined to pitch a no-hitter. Name these pitchers, their team, and when it happened.

22. Dizzy Dean was once hit on the head by a batted ball. At the hospital they took X-rays. How did the headlines report the results?

23. This Brooklyn high schooler was such a fine basketball player that he was given a scholarship to the University of Cincinnati. Baseball would have lost one of its most brilliant performers if he had continued his basketball career. Who is he?

24. Carl Hubbell won his last sixteen National League games in 1936. Carl won his first eight games in 1937. How many consecutive games did Hubbell win during his streak?

25. In the second All-Star game in 1935, Carl Hubbell struck out five players in a row. Name the five.

26. Why was Denton Tree Young called "Cy"?

27. Over 200,000 people turned out to watch this rookie pitch his first three games in the majors. In fact, 78,000 watched him blank the White Sox, 1-0, in his first major league start. What drew such a large crowd to see a rookie pitcher?

28. Nolan Ryan's fastball has been timed at 100+ miles per hours, yet using the same measuring device, this Yankee shortstop's throw was timed at 127 miles per hour. Who is the shortstop?

ANSWERS

1. *Grover Cleveland Alexander was named for President Grover Cleveland. President Cleveland was our twenty-second president. He was defeated for reelection but was elected when he ran for the third time, becoming our twenty-fourth president as well.*

2. *Jim Barr of the San Francisco Giants retired forty-one consecutive batters, equivalent to 13⅔ innings of perfect ball. Not one man reached first. This was spread over two games. In the first game he pitched on August 23, 1972, Jim retired the last twenty-one batters to face him. On the 29th of August, he retired the first twenty batters he faced.*

3. *Christy Mathewson's nickname was "Big Six." Before the advent of radio and TV, people were hard pressed for entertainment. One of the entertainments of that time was racing to a fire with the fire engines. The best fire engine in New York was known as "Big Six." So, New York's finest pitcher was given its name.*

A fan once addressed a letter to Mathewson by pasting a big "6" on an envelope and mailing it. It got to him.

4. *As "lanceurs." Montreal games are announced in both English and French.*

5. *The "Unknown Man of Baseball" is the pitcher who struck out Casey in "Casey at the Bat."*

6. *A pitcher is considered to have extraordinary control if he doesn't walk a batter in a game. Randy Jones and Christy Mathewson share the record of no walks in sixty-eight consecutive innings, the equivalent of 7½ games. Matty racked up this record for the New York Giants in 1913, Jones in 1976 with San Diego.*

7. *Bob Feller.*

8. *Bob Feller was sworn into the Navy by the undefeated heavyweight champion Gene Tunney. Bob missed nearly four seasons due to his Navy service.*

9. *Al Downing served up Hank Aaron's 715th home run. Tracy Stallard tossed number 61 to Roger Maris, and Tom Zachary fed Babe Ruth number 60.*

10. *All pitching prior to 1884 was underhanded.*

11. *Sandy Koufax is the youngest player ever elected to the Baseball Hall of Fame. Sandy was twenty-six years old when elected and is the only pitcher in baseball history with more strikeouts than innings pitched.*

12. *Lefty Grove's real full name was Robert Moses Grove. He was nicknamed "Mose." Lefty won baseball's first American League M.V.P. Award in 1931. His pitching career spanned the years 1925 through 1941. He pitched nine years for the Athletics and eight years for the Red Sox. He won exactly 300 games while losing 141.*

13. *Tom Seaver's first name is George. He was born in Fresno, California, November 17, 1944. Tom broke an eighty-six-year-old record by striking out ten consecutive batters. Tom shares the one nine-inning-game-strikeout record with Steve Carlton and Nolan Ryan with nineteen K's.*

14. *I hope that you are not confused by this, but another Tom (not Tom Seaver) holds the record for strikeouts in a single game. Washington pitcher Tom Cheney struck out twenty-one batters in a sixteen-inning game, against Baltimore, September 12, 1962.*

15. *William Arthur Cummings, known as "Candy" Cummings, developed the curveball. This inaugurated the most radical departure in pitching in the history of baseball.*

16. *The pitcher simply tosses the ball in the air. The ball comes to a full stop and returns to his hand. After reading this, you will probably feel like tossing the book.*

17. *It was Dizzy Dean who started the fire, Diz pitched in the majors from 1930 through 1947. The decline in Dizzy's career began in the 1937 All-Star game when Earl Averill hit a line drive that broke Dizzy's toe. Diz tried pitching before the toe was fully healed and strained his arm, and this, in effect, ended his career. He pitched in a part of one game in 1941 and part of a game in 1947, and that was it.*

18. *Burleigh Grimes, known affectionately as "Old Stubblebeard" was the last pitcher to throw the spitter—legally. The end came in 1934. Grimes managed the Dodgers in 1937 and 1938.*

19. *Christy Mathewson's three shutouts in three starts in the 1905 World Series will probably never be equaled.*

20. *Don Gullett says he remembers the seventy-two points he scored in one high school football game as the biggest thrill of his early athletic career.*

21. *On the last day of the 1975 baseball season, Vida Blue, Paul Lindblad, Rollie Fingers, and Glenn Abbott combined to pitch a no-hitter for the Oakland A's.*

22. *Dizzy was taken to the hospital after being hit in the head. The next day's headlines read, "X-Rays of Dean's Head, Show Nothing."*

23. *Sandy Koufax was the star high school cage man who won a scholarship to the University of Cincinnati for his basketball ability.*

24. *Carl Hubbell actually won seventeen in a row in 1936. He won a World Series game after the season ended.*

25. *In the 1934 All-Star game Carl Hubbell struck out Babe Ruth, Lou Gehrig, Jimmy Foxx, Al Simmons, and Joe Cronin in a row.*

26. *The reason we call Denton True Young "Cy" is that his fastball was described as being as fast and destructive as a cyclone. Warming up without a catcher, Denton threw baseballs against a wooden fence. Someone remarked that the fence looked as if a cyclone had struck it.*

27. *Satchel Paige, the oldest rookie in history, made his major league debut at the age of forty-one in 1948. But his reputation from the Negro Leagues preceded him; Joe DiMaggio, who played against Satch's team in exhibition games, said he was the best pitcher he ever faced.*

Leroy Robert Paige stopped pitching in the majors in 1953, only to return in 1965 to pitch one game for Kansas City. He was about fifty-nine when he made his last start.

In 1934 Paige started twenty-nine games in twenty-nine days with the Bismarck team, which reportedly won 104 out of 105 games. In an exhibition game he once struck out Rogers Hornsby, considered to be the greatest right-handed hitter of all time, five times.

28. *Nolan Ryan's fastball was timed at a little over 100 miles per hour, Bob Feller's at 98.6 miles per hour. An ex-Yankee shortstop, Mark Koenig, had a throw that was timed at 127 miles per hour! Koenig was the Yankee shortstop from 1925 to 1930. He appeared in five World Series.*